Speaking Listening Expression

3B

Korea's Most Reputable and Innovative English Language Program

SLE 3B
Third Edition

Published by Wit&Wisdom
Wit&Wisdom is the professional language publishing company of the PAGODA Education Group.
PAGODA Tower 1306-6, 7, Seocho-Dong,
Seocho-Gu, Seoul, Korea 137-855
www.pagodabook.com

Imprint | PAGODA Books

First published 2008
Seventh impression 2013
Printed in the Republic of Korea

ISBN 978-89-6281-388-3 (14740)

Publisher	Kyung-Sil Park
Editing Supervisor	Mi-ran Shin
Senior Writers	Jonathan Edwards, Scott McRae, Lloyd McWhirter, Andy Thompson, Zack Rodecap
Contributing Writers	Trevor Hande, Dean Beckman
Editors	Dong-hoon Lee, So-jung Kong, Mi-ran Lee
Photo Contributors	Jonathan Edwards, Blair Kitchener, Stewart Thom
Illustrator	Ki-Soo Kwon

To Our Students

Since 1985, Pagoda Academy has been developing its SLE program to be one of the most popular and effective conversational English programs in Korea. Since the beginning, the experience and observations of the Pagoda instructors have gone into all of the material designed for the SLE courses. With each successive version of the textbooks, the writers have tried to build on the strengths of previous versions, while reflecting changes in teaching methodology and input from both instructors and students. This book is no exception.

For the current version of the SLE 3 textbook, we have assumed that students should have already acquired a reasonably good foundation of practical knowledge regarding the most common aspects of English. Thus, as opposed to lower levels of the program that focus primarily on building familiarity with indispensable functions and structures, Level 3 focuses almost exclusively on expression - helping you to go beyond mere knowledge of the mechanics of English, to naturally develop a fluent command of conversational English. This is done by providing you with stimulating material and engaging activities to encourage you to practice expressing yourself on a wide variety of topics.

However, no book can promise to deliver noticeable improvement in your English ability. The reason is that in order to make improvements to your English fluency, you must practice speaking as much as possible, and no conversational English textbook can make you speak. We have done our best to produce a book full of interesting topics and activities that will get even the most reserved among you talking. However, a book, no matter how well-written, is still just a book. Only you can improve your English fluency. And to do that you must overcome your shyness, frustration, pride and fear of making mistakes, and make an effort to speak. This will challenge you to believe in yourself, and to take the Pagoda motto to heart:

"I Can Do It."

Book Format for Level 3B

Overall Format

Each of the twenty lessons in this textbook focuses on a different topic, all of which have been chosen because they are of interest to a wide range of Korean ESL students. The topics provide a focal point for each lesson, such that all of the vocabulary, reading passages, dialogues, conversation activities and discussion questions examine different aspects of the topic. Each lesson contains enough material to constitute approximately 2 hours of class time, and includes the following elements.

Lesson Format

Language Points

Each lesson is introduced by a list of vocabulary that have been chosen because they are useful for discussing the topic of the lesson. Although some or even all of these items may be familiar to you already, the reason for including them is not merely to check that you can recognize them, but to encourage you to practice using them. Try to create opportunities in class to use the items in this section.

Dialogue

Almost every lesson includes a dialogue. This conversation, which uses some of the expressions from the Language Points section, focuses on the topic of the lesson in some way. It also raises relevant issues that your instructor may choose to discuss. Recordings of the dialogues are available for use in class or for self-study.

Reading

In nearly every lesson, there are reading passages that relate to the topic of the lesson. They also deal with interesting aspects of the topics that you instructor may choose to discuss with you in class. Although the reading passages have been produced specifically for this textbook, an effort has made to write material that you would typically find in a variety of different real-life contexts. Recordings of the readings are also available.

Conversation Activities

Each lesson contains at least two conversation activities, designed to give you the opportunity to explore the topic of the lesson in different ways with your classmates and teacher.

Discussion Questions

At the end of each lesson, there is a list of questions dealing with many different sides of the topic. These have been designed to encourage you to express your opinions, share your experiences with the class, and spark conversation.

Goals for the Course

1. You should be more comfortable discussing:

a. the impression you make on other people, and the impressions people make on you (1)
b. educational values and the strengths and weaknesses of the education system in your country (2)
c. methods to break out of your regular routine and add excitement to your life (4)
d. examples of prejudice in your own culture, and solutions for overcoming the problem (6)
e. important choices that you have made or will be making in the future, and the priorities that you have set for your life (7)
f. changes that you will be experiencing as you grow older (8)
g. the merits of becoming independent (10)
h. past travel experiences, travel preferences, and future travel plans (11)
i. the good and bad habits of yourself and people around you (13)
j. beauty standards and the issue of cosmetic surgery (14)
k. the lies you have told, and have been told (16)
l. your idea of a perfect life and your expectations for your future (17)
m. your career and possible career paths (18)

2. You should be better able to perform the following verbal functions, including the ability to:

a. present and justify arguments on a range of issues (i.e., the pros and cons of different educational systems (2), the appropriate punishment for a range of crimes (5), the pros and cons of the death penalty/capital punishment (5), the appropriate response to cases of discrimination (6), the pros and cons of the military draft (19)
b. analyze moral dilemmas and negotiate solutions with classmates (3)
c. complain and be assertive without being rude in a range of awkward situations (15)

3B

Table of Contents

LESSON

1 Best Foot Forward

Language Points

to put one's best foot forward

I really want the job, so I'm going to put my best foot forward in the interview. I'm going to research the company thoroughly, practice a lot, and buy a new suit.

to make an impression / to make a good (great) first impression

In your first interview you made a good impression on the interviewers, so they have invited you for a second interview.

to break the ice / an icebreaker

Beginning a conversation with someone I don't know is difficult, so I try to break the ice by telling a joke.

to strike up a conversation

He is very sociable. He often strikes up a conversation with strangers.

to (really) hit it off (from the beginning)

They met for the first time at the party, and they hit it off from the beginning. They've been going out ever since.

to turn (someone) off / off-putting

I can't believe he showed up drunk for our blind date. That really turned me off!

to have a natural affinity with someone

We are from the same country, and we have the same personality. And he's so friendly, too. We seem to have a natural affinity.

to put on a show / to keep up a charade / to show your true character

He was so polite and kind when we first met, but he was just putting on a show. Now that I know him better I realize that he's rude and selfish. He is showing his true character. I hate him!

outward appearance

Outward appearances can be deceiving. On the inside people can be quite different than they appear to be on the outside.

to accentuate / to play up / to downplay

In the job interview he tried to accentuate his excellent education and downplay his lack of experience.

Dialogue

An exchange student has his first encounter with one of his classmates.

Derek: Hey, do you mind if I sit here?

Giuseppe: Uh...uh...n-no.

Derek: Is this the first course you've taken with Professor Burns?

Giuseppe: Uh...uh...yes.

Derek: Oh yeah? **You're in for a real treat.** He's a great lecturer. You're probably thinking, like, 'Oh, Intro to Molecular Biology. This is going to be a real snoozer.' But I'm telling you, he really makes it interesting.

Giuseppe: Oh.

Derek: My name's Derek, by the way. I'm actually a third year Chemistry major, but I took Professor Burns' Organic Chemistry class last semester, and I loved it, so I decided to take this one. What's your major?

Giuseppe: Biotechnology.

Derek: Oh, yeah? Wow, that's gotta be pretty tough. Are there lots of labs every week? We've got, like, four a week. I'm averaging about five hours sleep a night. But it's alright - I drink a lot of coffee.

Giuseppe: I...I'm sorry, but I am not speaking English well.

Derek: Hey, that's okay, man. Where are you from?

Giuseppe: Italy. Milan, Italy.

Derek: Oh, yeah? You guys **did wicked at soccer** in 2006. I watched every game. Did you celebrate on the street when Italy won?

Giuseppe: Derek. There is Professor.

Derek: Oh, right. Nice talking to ya. Maybe **I'll see ya around**...What was your name again?

Giuseppe: Giuseppe. Call me Giuseppe.

Comprehension

1. It seems like Derek is trying hard to **make a good first impression** by showing a lot of interest in Giuseppe. Do you think that this is the best way to make a good first impression? How might it be taken the wrong way?

2. Giuseppe seems more than a little shy. Do you often feel nervous when meeting someone for the first time? How about if they are a native English speaker?

3. It is said that **you only get one chance to make a good first impression**. Do you agree? Why or why not?

4. If a person you meet for the first time doesn't say much, do you usually think they are unfriendly, or that they don't like you, or do you just assume that they are shy?

5. Finding common interests, such as leisure activities and likes and dislikes, is the usual way to get a conversation off to a good start. What kinds of topics do you usually use to **break the ice**?

6. When, if ever, do you have opportunities to **strike up a conversation** with a stranger?

7. If you really **hit it off** with someone from the start, do you usually end up becoming good friends?

8. Most of us pre-judge others to some extent before we even talk to them. How accurately do you think we can judge people based on their appearance alone?

9. If you want to make a good first impression on a member of the opposite sex, what are some things that you should and shouldn't do? Do you have a special technique?

Activity A

First Impressions

Most people tend to make certain assumptions about others, even before interacting with them. Before getting to know your partner, rate them on the following categories ('First Impression'). Keep this hidden from your partner. Then have some introductory conversation together for at least five to ten minutes. Finally, rate your partner again on the same categories ('Second Impression') and see if your first impression has changed and, if so, how much ('Difference'). Afterwards, discuss the results with your partner.

1	2	3	4	5
not at all	slightly	moderately	quite	very

Category	First Impression	Second Impression	Difference (+ / -)
Conservative	1—2—3—4—5	1—2—3—4—5	
Extroverted	1—2—3—4—5	1—2—3—4—5	
Easy-going	1—2—3—4—5	1—2—3—4—5	
Ambitious	1—2—3—4—5	1—2—3—4—5	
Charismatic	1—2—3—4—5	1—2—3—4—5	

1. What evidence served as the basis for your first impression of your partner? What, for example, made you think that your partner was or was not conservative? Check the categories below that apply.

- ☐ Style of dress
- ☐ Hairstyle / makeup
- ☐ Tone and volume of voice
- ☐ Other
- ☐ Facial expression
- ☐ Body language
- ☐ Amount of eye contact

2. Discuss the impressions you generally form based on each of the above categories. For example, how might you judge a person dressed in smart casual dress compared to someone dressed in jeans and a t-shirt?
3. Apart from the above categories, can you think of any other cues that you use to form opinions of people you meet for the first time?
4. Compared to your partner's image of him or herself, how accurate was your first impression?
5. How many of our first impressions are formed consciously and how many do you think are formed subconsciously?
6. What is it that makes you dislike a person the first time you meet them? What sorts of people **turn you off** right away?
7. What sorts of people do you **have a natural affinity with** as soon as you meet them?

Activity B

Self-monitoring

When you first meet someone, how concerned are you about the impression you make? Nearly everyone tries to **put their best foot forward** when meeting others for the first time. However, some people consciously try to control themselves and monitor their behavior more than others. '**Self-monitoring**' refers to the extent to which you control the nonverbal signals that you send to others and the degree to which you adjust your behavior based on the particular situation you are in. High self-monitors are particularly talented in this way compared to low self-monitors. Complete the following scale to find out how hard you work on your self-presentation.

If a statement is TRUE or MOSTLY TRUE, write "T" next to it. If a statement is FALSE or NOT USUALLY TRUE, write "F" next to it.

1. I find it hard to imitate the behavior of other people.
2. At parties and social events, I don't try to do or say things that others will like.
3. I can only argue for ideas I already believe in.
4. I guess I **put on a show** to impress or entertain people.
5. I would probably make a good actor.
6. I rarely need the advice of my friends to choose movies, books, or music.
7. I laugh more when I watch a comedy with others than when alone.
8. In a group of people, I am rarely the center of attention.
9. In different situations and with different people, I often act differently.
10. I am not particularly good at making other people like me.
11. Even if I am not enjoying myself, I often pretend to be having a good time.

☐	**12.** I would not change my opinions (or the way I do things) to please someone.
☐	**13.** At a party, I let others keep the jokes and stories going.
☐	**14.** I can look anyone in the eye and tell a lie with a straight face.
☐	**15.** I may deceive people by being friendly when I really dislike them.

Scoring: The scoring key is reproduced below. You should circle your response of true or false each time it corresponds to the keyed response below. Add up the number of responses you circle. This total is your score on the Self-Monitoring Scale. Record your score below.

1. False	2. False	3. False	4. True	5. True
6. False	7. True	8. False	9. True	10. False
11. True	12. False	13. False	14. True	15. True

How many matching answers did you have? ______________

Score Interpretation:

10 - 15	High self-monitor	
6 - 9	Intermediate self-monitor	
0 - 5	Low self-monitor	

Discussion

1. How important do you think **first impressions** really are? Why do you think so?
2. Can you think of a time when you **made a great first impression** on somebody? How did it help you?
3. Do you think that people who are good at impression management (changing their behavior to suit the situation) are generally more successful than those who are not?
4. Do you think that a person who uses impression management a lot finds it difficult to act naturally?
5. In what situations do you think **making a good first impression** is particularly important?
6. Eventually a person will show their true character to other people. So, do you think that it is better to behave naturally in front of other people from the start? Why or why not?
7. It is often said that many people 'change' after marriage and reveal another side of their personality that their spouse doesn't like. Do you think that co-habitation before marriage is a good way to find out what a person is really like?
8. Can you usually tell when a person is **putting on a show** for other people?

9. To what extent do you think that it is acceptable to bend the truth to make a good first impression?

10. Most people lie to some extent on their job application form. Does the fact that most people do this make it acceptable or not?

11. It is well-known that many people lie about themselves when they enter an Internet 'chat-room'. Would you be naturally skeptical about personal information that you received from someone you met on-line?

12. It is said that 'clothes make the man'. To what extent do you usually judge people according to their clothing?

13. Are people from your country quick to judge people based on the clothes that they wear? In this regard, are people from your country more (or less)judgmental than people from other countries?

14. Is it wrong to judge people based on their **outward appearance**? Or do **outward appearances** really say a lot about someone's character?

15. Would you be likely to form a different impression of your English teacher if he / she wore casual clothes rather than a suit? Would you naturally assume that an English teacher who wore a suit was better in some way than a teacher who wore casual clothes?

16. At what age do you think we start to be concerned with the impression that we make on other people? At what age, if ever, do we stop being so concerned about it?

17. If nobody cared about the impression they made on others, do you think that the world would be a better or worse place? Why do you think so?

18. "Everything that irritates us about others can lead us to an understanding of ourselves." - Carl Jung (1875 - 1961) What does this mean? Do you agree or disagree?

19. If you were trying to impress a member of the opposite sex, which aspect(s) of yourself would you try to **accentuate**? What aspect(s) would you try to **downplay**?

20. When a person spends excessive amounts of money on designer clothes and accessories, what kind of impression do you think they are trying to make? Do you think that such people are sometimes trying to mask some character weaknesses?

21. It is said that 'you can't judge a book by its cover'. To what extent do you agree with this expression? How long should you spend getting to know a person before you draw conclusions about them?

22. Comment on the following quote: "You can make more friends in two months by becoming interested in other people than you can in two years by trying to get other people interested in you." - Dale Carnegie

23. Through the years, we have received advice on how to make an impression on people. Discuss the meaning of these quotations, each of which deals with making a good impression on people. To what extent do you agree with the statement/saying? Will each piece of advice help you make a good impression on people?

- "Humor is the great thing, the saving thing. The minute it crops up, all our irritations and resentments slip away and a sunny spirit takes their place." - Mark Twain
- "Remember that a person's name is to that person the sweetest and most important sound in any language." -Dale Carnegie
- "No matter what a woman looks like, if she's confident, she's sexy." –Paris Hilton
- "The man who has confidence in himself gains the confidence of others." –Hasidic saying
- "The apparel often proclaims the man." –Shakespeare
- "Dress for where you are going, not from where you have been." –A common saying

LESSON

2 The More, the Better?

Language Points

clique / cliquey

Some people at my high school were very cliquey. They spent time only with people that belonged to their clique and were a little unfriendly towards people who were outside of it.

an old acquaintance

I am so glad that I went to my high school reunion. I saw many old acquaintances that I had not seen in years.

to be picked on by a bully

When he was young he was small and weak, so he was often picked on by the schoolyard bully.

to get back in touch (with someone)

I'd like to get back in touch with some of my friends from high school. I wonder what they've been doing. I miss them.

extracurricular (activities, clubs, sports)

He does so many extracurricular activities. He is on the basketball team, in the acting club, and in the student government. I don't know how he ever finds time to study for exams.

to have a crush on (someone)

When I was a high school freshman, I had a crush on a pretty girl in my math class. But I was very shy, so I never asked her out on a date.

a cram school

Many students go to cram schools after their regular high school classes have finished. They think that they can get much higher test scores by going there.

the real world

Some things that I learned in school were worthless in the real world. I have never used the information at work or in my relationships.

to play a prank (on someone)

I'll never forget the time we played a prank on my math teacher. We placed a tack on his chair. When he sat down on it, he screamed so loud you could hear him all over the school.

Dialogue

Two former classmates bump into each other at a bar.

Randy: Arnold? Arnold Blaine is that you? Geez! I hardly recognized you with that beard. How long has it been? Like 20 years?

Arnold: Hey Randy. Yup...21 years. How time flies, eh? So, what've you been up to? I guess you're married...kids...the whole bit.

Randy: Yeah, sure, I did the marriage thing... but well, you know how it goes...it didn't last too long. Actually, Sheryl and I have been divorced for almost five years. Anyways, I'm working at...

Arnold: Sheryl? Sheryl Walker?! I remember her. Man, you married her? I didn't think she was your type.

Randy: (a little angry) Uh...What do you mean...exactly ? We dated all through graduating year. I thought you knew about that.

Arnold: No, I had no idea! I mean, you were a **football jock**. She was one of those **artsy** chicks, always dressed in black, **moping** around, listening to all that depressing music. It's just sort of surprising.

Randy: Well, you can't always judge a book by its cover. Getting to know Sheryl made me realize that.

Arnold: Your friends must have given you a hard time, you know, dating such a **weirdo**.

Randy: (Angrier) Not really. I didn't really care that much what they thought. They were all pretty shallow and materialistic. You know...typical **preppies**. Anyways, how about...

Arnold: Not all preppies are **superficial** and **materialistic**, you know, Randy. You probably didn't really know any of the people in my **clique**. Am I right?

Randy: No. I guess we didn't really swim in the same circles.

Arnold: Well, good seeing you again, Randy. Take it easy.

Randy: Yeah, sure. Take it easy...

Comprehension

1. When Randy bumps into Arnold, it is not long before they begin stereotyping each other as if they were back in high school. If you bump into someone who you haven't seen for a very long time, do you tend to treat them in the same way as when you first knew them?

2. If you saw someone you recognized as **an old acquaintance**, would you feel embarrassed to go up to them and say hello? How about an old girlfriend or boyfriend?

3. Have you ever **got back in touch with** any old school friends whom you hadn't seen in ages? Did you meet face to face and, if so, were they similar to how you remembered them?

4. When you were back in school, did you usually hang out with members of a particular social group? What other social groups do you remember? Did you tend to **look down on other groups** or have some negative stereotypes about them?

5. Randy got married to his high school sweetheart. Do you know anyone who got married to their **high school sweetheart**? If so, was it successful?

6. If you ran into someone you used to dislike after many years, would you just ignore them or give them another chance to show they had changed?

7. Do you agree with Randy that '**you can't always judge a book by its cover**'? Did you ever pre-judge someone and then, after getting to know them, find out that your first impressions were totally wrong?

Activity A

Are School Uniforms Outdated?

Many schools in Western countries don't require their students to wear uniforms. A lot of students (and parents) think that school uniforms are outdated and irrelevant. However, many people still think that 'you behave the way you're dressed' and some schools that re-introduced a uniform policy found it beneficial.

With your partner(s), adopt one of the following positions and, after having read the points listed below, debate whether or not students should be made to wear a uniform.

POSITION ONE Keeping uniforms	POSITION TWO Getting rid of uniforms
• Improves the school atmosphere, making it a better place to learn • Helps reduce ethnic and racial differences between students • Helps reduce the apparent gap between rich and poor students • Reduces the burden on parents to buy expensive clothes for fashion-conscious children • Improves discipline and reduces tardiness • Encourages students to study harder	• Allows students freedom of expression • Helps students relax and be more creative • Relieves parents of the extra hassle of buying uniforms for their kids • Relieves the burden on teachers of enforcing dress codes • Helps students develop a sense of self-identity from an early age • Encourages students to identify with certain groups, forming strong social bonds

Activity B

Hindsight Is 20 / 20

The expression 'hindsight is 20 / 20' means that, after looking back on past events, it's easy to see how certain situations in the past could have been improved. Just by changing a few things, our lives could have been much happier, easier or more successful. With your classmate(s), think about some changes that could have made your school or university days better.

Could you have.....

- spent more time hanging out with friends instead of wasting time studying certain subjects that turned out to be useless for your future?
- avoided certain people or situations that ended up getting you into trouble?

Should you have.....

- plucked up the courage to ask a certain guy or girl out on a date?
- taken part in more **extracurricular clubs** and activities?

How might.....

- things have been different if you'd had a different **circle of friends**?
- things have been better if you'd studied a different major?

How would.....

- your life have been easier if you'd listened to your teachers' and parents' advice?
- your experience of school life have been better if you'd simply had a different attitude?

Activity C

Devil's Advocate

Sometimes, in order to stimulate discussion or force someone to justify his or her opinion, we might take an opposing view, even if that is not necessarily what we believe. This is called 'playing devil's advocate'. With your partner, take turns being the devil's advocate. One student will state his/her opinion, and the other will contradict it for the purpose of debate. Do you agree that....

1. Schools are generally effective at developing students' intelligence.

2. Some physical discipline is good for students.

3. Students can learn everything they need from school, so hiring private tutors or attending **cram schools** is a waste of money.

4. Schools prepare students for the challenges they will face in the real world.

5. A student who studies most of the night and sleeps only three hours will get into a better university than a student who studies less and sleeps six hours.

6. High school students should be allowed to choose the courses they take.

7. The government is to blame for most of the problems in the education system.

8. Achieving a high G.P.A. at the end of your degree should be more important than the name of the university you attend.

9. Coeducation is superior to single-sex education because it provides a better educational experience and understanding of the opposite sex.

10. Simply memorizing large amounts of material from textbooks is not an effective way to learn.

Discussion

Reminiscing About Our School Days

1. How would you describe your **social circle** in high school? What kinds of students did you associate with? What kinds did you dislike?
2. Usually the most popular guys in North American high schools are good athletes. The most popular girls are stylish and sociable. What kind of people were the most popular in your school? What kinds of people were considered 'losers'? Were you popular in your class?
3. **The prom** – a formal dance held near the end of the academic year – is the most important social even of the year in most American high schools. What was the most important social event in your school?
4. Did you get involved in any **extracurricular** activities? Were you involved in your school's student government?
5. Some people's high school experiences affect them for many years afterward. What was the most memorable thing that happened to you in high school (good or bad)? What is something you will never forget? What would you like to forget?
6. Have you ever had a **reunion** with your former classmates? Do you think they have changed much? Do you think you have changed much? How?
7. In elementary school and high school, were you ever **picked on by a bully**? What happened? Did you ever bully weaker or younger students? What did you do to them?
8. Did you have a boyfriend / girlfriend during your high school years?
9. Did you ever **have a crush on** one of your teachers?
10. At what point during your teenage years did you feel like you were no longer a child? Why?
11. If your high school classmates had voted for you in one of the following categories, which one would they have chosen? Who from this class best fits these categories?

Best looking	Funniest	Craziest	Most likely to succeed	Smartest
Most Athletic	**Friendliest**	**Most popular**	**Toughest**	**Laziest**

12. Did you used to feel '**burned-out**' from studying too many hours? Do you think that you could have got as much benefit from studying less but more intensively?
13. Did you have a private tutor or attend a **cram school** when you were younger? If so, do you feel that you really benefited from it?
14. Did you ever **play pranks** on any of your teachers? What was the funniest prank you can remember? How did the teacher react? Did you get punished afterwards?

15. Were you able to motivate yourself to study long hours during your high school years? How many hours per day did you used to study on average? Did your parents ever try to force you to study more?
16. What was your school's policy regarding alcohol and smoking? Did you ever get into trouble for engaging in either of the above activities? What was your punishment?
17. Do you remember any famous cases at a school you attended in which students were disciplined or expelled for bad behavior?

The Education System and Classroom Learning

1. What are the strengths and weaknesses of the education system in your country? What are your recommendations for improvements?
2. What differences are you aware of between the education system in your home country and another country that you are familiar with?
3. What aspects of the US or UK education systems should be introduced to your home country? What aspects of your home country's education system should be introduced to the US or the UK?
4. Are high school students in your country encouraged to express their opinions in class? Are creativity and originality stressed? Should there be more focus on these skills / values?
5. Were you allowed to choose the courses you took? Should high school students have more freedom to choose their courses? What subjects should be required? How about religion, art, music and sex education?
6. In the US, students entering university are required to take the Scholastic Aptitude Test (SAT). In your country, are students who wish to attend university required to take an entrance exam? Did the test put a lot of pressure on you? Did preparing for the exam ruin your high school experience? Why or why not?
7. Is there a particular teacher who you especially remember from high school or university? If so, what was so special about him or her?
8. Was there a teacher who inspired you and influenced you in some important way?
9. What are the qualities of good teachers? Consider values, teaching styles, and personality traits.
10. "Sometimes failure is the best teacher a student could have." Talk about a time in which you learned from failure. What did you learn, and why?

LESSON

3 Conscience

Language Points

one's conscience

I feel bad about saying such unkind things to him. I want to apologize to him. It's been on my conscience.

a rationale

I often take pencils, pens and erasers from work. My rationale is that my company doesn't pay me enough for the work that I do. They owe me something, so I don't feel guilty.

a worrywart

I never steal anything because I'm a worrywart, so I'm always afraid that I'm going to get caught.

an ethical dilemma

I have an ethical dilemma. An Internet shopping site thinks I have paid for my new MP3 player. Actually, I haven't. Should I keep quiet and accept the MP3 player without actually paying, or should I point out the mistake and send the money?

to fess up

Everyone knows you stole the money from her. Why don't you fess up?

to plagiarize

He got caught plagiarizing material from the Internet, so he received an "F" on his paper.

to fiddle (taxes/expenses/figures)

Fiddling your expenses is risky for employees because most companies check their expenses closely.

to help oneself to (something)

I was in the office alone, so I helped myself to several packages of A4 paper and many company pencils and pens. I put them in my bag and took them home.

to feel remorse / remorseful

What I did was wrong and unethical. I feel remorseful.

to stick to your principles

My friends put pressure on me to do something I knew was wrong, but I stuck to my principles and I didn't do it.

Dialogue

Two good friends are alone at the office working overtime.

Barry: (Laughing) Hey Paul! I just found the key to the supply room.

Paul: You did! It's our lucky day because I need to get a couple of cartridges for my printer at home and the kids need loads of supplies for school; you know, notebooks, pens, sticky notes, and maybe a couple of packages of computer paper.

Barry: You're not serious, are you? I know we're alone, but I'm a little nervous about **helping myself to** the company's supplies.

Paul: Come on. Don't worry so much. This is a big company. They can afford it and nobody will miss a few supplies. Besides I think we're both good workers and we should be paid more then we are getting. I think of this as **a fringe benefit**.

Barry: But isn't it stealing?

Paul: Not really. We worked for it! Like I said, it's a fringe benefit.

Barry: That's the same **rationale** you used when we **padded** our overtime hours. I remember you told me to always add a few hours to **compensate** for the time away from my friends. I'm still worried that the people in the payroll department will find out somehow.

Paul: Don't be such a **worrywart**. There's no way anyone can find out about it unless you say something. Besides, everybody does it.

Barry: No, Paul, everyone doesn't do it.

Paul: Well, everyone should because most companies don't pay their employees enough for what they do.

Barry: Hey, isn't that the boss coming out of the elevator?

Paul: You're right! Let's look busy.

Barry: Whew! What would have happened if we had had those supplies on our desks when he went by?

Paul: I think **our days would have been numbered**. You'd better put that key back where you found it before the boss sees you with it.

Barry: I can't, I found it on his desk along with these other keys.

Paul: You idiot! That's why he came back - to get his car keys. Now what?!

Comprehension

1. Who's opinion do you agree with more, Barry's or Paul's? Justify your opinion.

2. Have you ever **helped yourself to** company or school supplies? What kind of stuff did you take?

3. Do you think that taking supplies from a large company is more acceptable than taking supplies from a small company? Explain your rationale.

4. If you were in a low paid job, would you feel less guilty about **helping yourself to** company supplies? Can this be considered a 'company perk?'

5. Morally, do you think there is any difference between taking supplies from a company and stealing from a store?

6. Have you ever been caught stealing? Did you **feel remorseful** afterwards or were you just sorry that you got caught?

7. Do you agree with Paul when he says that most companies don't pay their employees enough for what they do? Have you ever felt exploited by your employer?

8. If a friend tries to persuade you to do something that is **against your conscience**, do you tend to be easily persuaded or do you usually **stick to your principles**?

9. If there was no danger of getting caught and everyone else did it, would you take supplies from your from your company, school, etc., with a free and easy mind?

10. If a company treats its employees fairly, do you think this is likely to cut down on internal theft?

Activity A

Ethical Dilemmas

Discuss with your classmate(s) what you would do if faced with the following ethical dilemmas. Would you try to make the most of the opportunity or would you obey your conscience? Give reasons to support your choice. If your conversation partner(s) disagrees with you, try to convince him or her that you are right.

1 You have noticed two of your colleagues and long-time friends taking various items from the office. At your company, not only theft, but also failure to report theft, can both result in dismissal. Your friends have ignored your warnings and the boss is due to take a stock inventory tomorrow. What should you do?

2 Your son has been getting a lot of punishment from his teacher lately. You've heard that other parents pay bribe money to this particular teacher. On one hand, you are really against this kind of practice but, on the other hand, you don't want your son to be treated unfairly. What should you do?

3 Your boss invites you and some other co-workers to a so-called gentleman's club after work. From your previous experience, you know that things often get pretty wild. However, since the last time you went, you have got married and you know that your spouse would strongly disapprove. On the other hand, your boss won't accept no for an answer. What would you do?

4 You are studying for your up-coming university entrance exam and your parents are pressuring you to get into a good university. However, you are really worried that you will get a low grade because you haven't studied enough. A few days before the exam a friend tells you that they have managed to obtain a copy of the exam paper. Would you ask your friend to let you see the paper?

5 Your boss told you that one of your co-workers is among several to be laid off soon. You were told not to tell your co-worker yet as he might spread the news which would cause an outrage. Meanwhile you heard from you co-worker that he's intending to buy a new car and pay for his wife to have a nose job. What should you do?

6 You are working your part-time job at a bar and, at the end of the night, you find a cheap jacket that has been left behind by a customer. It doesn't seem to belong to a regular customer and when you check the pockets, you find nothing except a plain envelope with $1000 inside. Your job is not well paid and you could really use the money to pay an urgent debt.

7 You are a project team leader and one of your young team members (who happens to be your boss' daughter) has a problem with body odor. It seems that this is not a medical problem. If you tell the girl that her body odor is offensive she will probably quit in shame and complain to her father. On the other hand, other team members are threatening to quit if you don't do something about it.

8 You work for a branch of an American multinational. Your manager, who is American, is always talking down to you and you feel that it is only because of your nationality. If you complain, you could lose your job. However, you can't take much more and are about to snap. How should you handle this situation?

Activity B

Fess Up

Read the following situations and discuss which of the three options is the right thing to do, which is the wrong thing to do, and which is simply avoiding the problem. Then discuss which one you would (honestly) choose and why.

Situation	Option 1	Option 2	Option 3
❶ You have to submit your thesis by tomorrow but the only way is to **plagiarize material** from the Internet.	Cut and paste. Get it in on time, and hope you don't get caught.	Write original material, but hand it in late and have marks deducted.	Call your instructor and make up an excuse to buy more time.

2 You've heard your co-workers **spreading nasty rumors** that could seriously hurt other people if they were ever revealed.	Go directly to the management and inform them who **the offenders** are.	Anonymously inform the victims of the rumors who has been spreading the rumors.	Try to get a transfer to another department.
3 You're really short of money and your accountant has pointed out a way to **fiddle your taxes** and save $2000.	Dismiss your accountant and find one who can save you at least $4000.	Say you want things done legally, but the more he saves you, the more you'll pay him.	Tell your accountant to find another job and hire an honest person instead.
4 Your friend's son has been selected for a scholarship. However, your son claims he saw him cheating on a test. If this fact is exposed your son has a chance to get the scholarship instead.	Reveal the boy's dishonesty to the authorities and claim the scholarship for your son.	Approach your friend and urge him or her to do the right thing.	Congratulate your friend's son on getting the scholarship.
5 You are in charge of production at a toy doll manufacturing company. You are well behind schedule and in danger of losing your bonuses and maybe even your job. If you skip the safety checks you can meet your targets.	Skip the safety checks, and hope no one finds out. No one will get hurt.	Talk to your manager and get him to extend your deadlines so that you have time to do the job properly. Give up your bonuses.	Motivate your staff to work harder, doing overtime if necessary, to meet the deadline.
6 You are applying for a job that you really want. It's down to just you and another guy you know. However, you happen to know that he has lied extensively on his resume.	Lie in your interview to level the playing field.	Reveal the deception and get the job.	Keep your mouth shut and count on your own merit to get you the job.

Activity C

Virtuous Reality

As a guide to morally acceptable behavior, many people used to refer to the list of virtues. A virtue is a good quality or way of behaving. Discuss some of the following virtues.

- Which ones are still relevant and which are not?
- How are they relevant?
- Can you think of some situations in which these virtues are still important?
- Are some of these virtues unrealistic in today's world?

Politeness
good manners; socially acceptable behavior; not being rude

Fidelity
loyalty to a person, organization or set of beliefs

Prudence
showing care and good sense when acting or making decisions

Temperance
doing things in moderation; avoiding excess

Justice
fairness in the way that people are treated

Generosity
doing or giving more than is usual or expected

Mercy
choosing not to harm or punish someone you have power over

Courage
doing something difficult or dangerous despite your fear

Gratitude
thanking someone for something they have done or given to you

Humility
being modest; not believing that you are better than someone else

Simplicity
keeping things simple so that it can be done or understood easily

Tolerance
allowing others to do and say as they like even if you disapprove

Purity
following what you know to be morally acceptable behavior

Gentleness
acting in a calm and controlled manner with little force

Discussion

1. Is there anything you've done that you **regret**? Is there anything you can do to improve the situation?
2. After doing something you know is wrong, do you usually try to **justify your actions to yourself**? What are some of the ways you can do this?
3. Have you ever faced an **ethical dilemma** at work or at school? What was the dilemma? How did you **resolve the dilemma**? Did you talk to anyone to help you make your decision?
4. Did you ever **fess up** after someone accused you of doing something wrong? What happened? Why did you **confess**?
5. Have you recently made up an excuse about something wrong that you have done? Did you make the excuse to your boss/manager? Your mother or father? Girlfriend, boyfriend, wife, or husband? A teacher or professor?
6. Where do you think we get our sense of right and wrong?
7. Why do you think most people have **a conscience**? Do you have a strong conscience? Give reasons to support your answer.
8. Do you consider yourself **an ethical person**? Do you always try to be **ethical**, or are you 'flexible' about some things? Why or why not?
9. Some people do things that they know are wrong only because others also do. In English, we call this 'peer pressure' or 'social pressure'. Why do you think people sometimes follow the crowd?
10. How did your parents teach you right from wrong?
11. To some people, the same action may be right in one situation and wrong in another. That is to say, they think that ethics are 'relative'. Can you think of any examples in which the same action might be right in one situation but wrong in another?
12. Are you optimistic or pessimistic about human nature? Do you think that people generally try to do the right thing, or do most people **try to get away with** as much as they can? Give reasons to explain your opinion.
13. Do you believe that people who try hard to be good will ultimately be rewarded for their efforts? What makes you think so?
14. Is there anyone you know who is especially **ethical**? Give an example of something they did that gave you this impression. Would you like to try to be like this person?
15. Altruism is the act of helping other people even though there is no benefit for ourselves. Do you believe that there is such a thing as real altruism, or do people simply do such things to feel better about themselves?
16. Who is responsible for teaching and upholding **moral and ethical behavior**; our parents, our teachers, the government, or someone else?
17. Do you always find it easy to distinguish between right and wrong? How about when the thing that is wrong is very advantageous to you?

18. Do you think that those who are wealthy or in positions of power such as politicians have a greater responsibility to behave in morally and ethically correct ways?

19. "When people behave in immoral or **unethical ways**, it is usually because there is a lot of temptation to do so." To what extent do you agree or disagree with this statement?

20. Do you think that it is unfair to criticize others for behaving badly in certain situations unless we have first faced the same situation ourselves and done the right thing?

21. Are there any high-profile cases of famous people (politicians, businessmen, celebrities, etc.) **fessing up** to doing something wrong? What happened? What did they **confess to**? Why do you think they confessed?

22. What would be an appropriate punishment for a student found guilty of **plagiarism**? Should the student fail the assignment? Fail the course? Be suspended for a semester? Why?

23. Should celebrities be allowed to sue people who **spread nasty, unfounded rumors** about them on the Internet?

LESSON

4 Bored Stupid

Language Points

a monotonous/mundane/stagnant/tedious routine

My life is monotonous. Every day I follow the same tedious routine. I get up, go to work, come home, eat dinner, use the Internet for a while, and then go to bed. Nothing ever changes.

restless

I've been working the same job for five years, and I'm starting to feel restless and impatient. I think I need to change jobs.

to crave excitement

I spend all day every day working a boring job, so these days I am really craving excitement. I'm starving for it.

to venture out

Why are we staying here in the apartment? I think we should venture out and do something interesting and exciting.

vicarious / to live vicariously through (someone) / to experience something vicariously

Some parents live vicariously through their children. They experience joy when they see their children doing things that they didn't have the chance to do.

living on the edge

I know a guy who really loves extreme sports. His favorite sports are skydiving and parasailing. He loves the excitement of living on the edge.

to live life to the fullest

I believe in living life to the fullest, so every day I get up early and try to do a lot of things. I have a lot of hobbies and passions.

a thrill-seeker / a risk-taker / to take risks

I'm not a thrill-seeker. I never play extreme sports or do anything risky. Actually, I lead quite an unexciting life.

adrenaline / an adrenaline rush / an adrenaline junkie

I love skiing and other exciting sports because they give me an adrenaline rush.

Reading

Bored in a Sea of Entertainment

Just as polar bears and other animals with advanced nervous systems exhibit abnormal behaviour and signs of stress when permanently housed in small barren cages, humans also experience stress when their lives become **monotonous**. Whenever we start to feel **restless**, fidgety and irritable, uninterested in work, school, or hobbies, we naturally tend to **crave excitement**, novelty, and a break from the **mundane routine** of daily life.

The **sense of urgency** with which we try to avoid feelings of boredom has an evolutionary function. The feeling of boredom is triggered by a lack of stimulation or by the repetitiveness of activities, and thus it pushes both animals and humans to break out of **stagnant** cycles of behaviour by adapting, **venturing out**, developing in new ways, and learning new things about their environment. Boredom, in this sense, has moved culture onwards; it has brought about new technological innovations, as well as works of art and entertainment.

In many cases, people try to escape feelings of boredom by seeking stimulation in the form of strong emotional reactions - anger, fear, love, sexual arousal, disgust, even sadness. People deliberately expose themselves to fear in the form of extreme sports, roller coasters, action and horror movies. Others **vicariously** satisfy their drive for aggression and anger through violence on television, movies or video games. Many people also become involved in the emotional scenarios of soap operas or movies, and despite their powerful effects, some people seek out sadness and drama to keep from being bored. Producers in the mass media deliberately prey upon the public's need for stimulation. The news media's fixation with sensational murders is an example of its exploitation of this need. Most films feature violence as the basis for attracting an audience, as do many television programs whose theme is crime.

However, as people become increasingly exposed to high levels of violence or sexual content in the media, they become accustomed or desensitized to it. With repeated exposure, the same kind of content no longer provokes the same sort of reaction, so people often seek stimulation in more extreme forms. Nearly eighty-four percent of Americans in the 19 - 55 age bracket believe that today's TV programs are boring. Seventy-one percent believe the same about big-budget movies.

But equally, the danger of more **sinister** responses to boredom is always **lurking**. Seeking release from boredom is a factor that, in part, can explain widespread social problems and destructive behaviours. Boredom has been linked to everything from compulsive buying, gambling, eating disorders, and drug and alcohol abuse, to violent crime, suicide, sexual promiscuity and adultery.

Our society has developed to the point where many of our basic survival needs are met, and yet, biologically our species is still programmed with the drives that would have aided us in our survival hundreds or thousands of years ago. Just like captive polar bears, whose hunting instincts drive them to pace back and forth endlessly, we may be driven by **deep-seated** instincts, to overcome our boredom by stimulating our **primal** emotions in a variety of ways. As life becomes more and more controlled and routine, and we become increasingly desensitized to the stimulations that are offered to us by the media, who can imagine what sorts of diversions and entertainment we will see in the future?

Comprehension

1. Have you ever seen large animals in the zoo? Describe their behaviour.
2. In what ways are we like animals in the ways we respond to boredom?

3. At the end of the article, the author makes a dire prediction about the future of media. Speculate about some of the things we can expect to see in the future in movies, television, the news, etc.
4. When you are bored, what are you likely to do for a little excitement?
5. **Monotony** or **routine** seems to bother people to varying degrees. Why do you think some people are driven to extreme behaviour by boredom, whereas other people are quite content to live a relatively unexciting life?
6. When you consider your own behaviour after reading this article, do you think anything that you do might be an attempt to escape boredom?
7. How can we deal with boredom in healthy ways?
8. Can you think of any common situations that you find intolerably boring? What do you normally do to make them a little more interesting?
9. Do you agree with the idea that our craving for excitement is biologically controlled? If so, is it then impossible to control?
10. If there were no aggressive movies or video games to help satisfy our appetite for violence, do you think that there would be more violent crime?

Activity A

Taking Your Chances

Look at the following list of activities. Rate them according to how risky you consider each of them relative to the others. Then indicate which you would be willing to try, and which you'd be unwilling to. Discuss the questions below with your classmate(s).

Rating

Very Risky				Moderately Risky				Not Risky at All	
1	2	3	4	5	6	7	8	9	10

Rating	Would you be willing to try it?	Yes	No
	Driving in excess of 180 km / h		
	Scuba diving		
	Swimming in a lake at night		
	Traveling to a foreign country by yourself		
	Wrestling a professional wrestler		
	Sleeping in the woods by yourself		
	Asking a complete stranger out on a date		
	Giving a speech in front of a crowd of 300 people		
	Riding a motorcycle in a big, busy city		
	Holding a venomous snake		
	Having a conversation with a homeless person		
	Making a complaint at a restaurant		
	Being a contestant on a television game show		

Discussion

1. What is it about the activities you'd be unwilling to try that makes you feel most uncomfortable?
2. Based on the results of this activity, do you consider yourself an adventurous or an unadventurous person?
3. Do any of the above activities appeal to you? Why or why not?
4. Explain what the following quotes mean. Which one do you agree with more?
   a. No man is unhappier than the one who is never in difficulty; the greatest affliction of life is never to be afflicted. - Victor Hugo
   b. Every step of life shows much caution is required. - Johann Wolfgang Von Goethe
5. What is better in your opinion, a safe, **mundane** life or a dangerous, exciting one? Why?
6. Would you ever consider going bungee jumping or skydiving? Give reasons.

Activity B

Organize a Recreational Sports Club

Imagine that you and your classmate(s) are planning to organize a recreational sports club. Discuss and decide on the following issues and prepare to give a presentation about your club to the class.

1. What sport(s) will you play? When? Where? How often?
2. Who will be admitted into your club?
3. What criteria will you use to choose your club members?
4. Should all your members be athletes?
5. Can professionals join your club?
6. Will members be subject to a registration or membership fee? If yes, how often will they be expected to pay it?
7. Who will you compete with? Will you be part of any leagues already existing or will you start up your own league?
8. Will men and women compete together?
9. Will there be any regular social activities held by the club? What kind?
10. What will the name of your club be?

Now give a promotional presentation about your club to the class.

Activity C

Living on the Edge

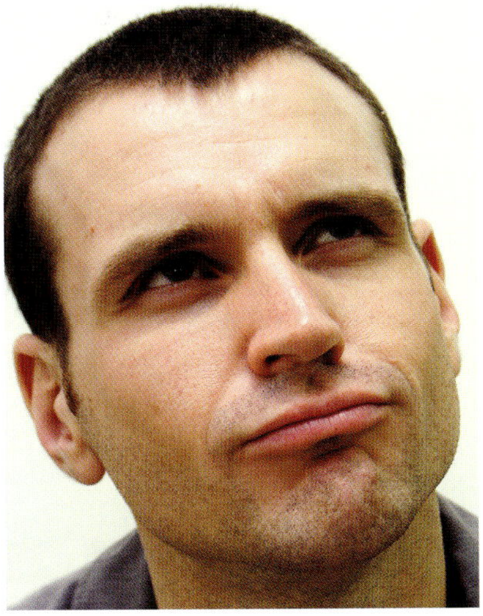

Do you seek a variety of new and interesting experiences, or do you prefer the tried and true? For each of the 14 choices, choose the conservative option or the adventurous option. Check the option you choose. Try to explain why you prefer one option over the other. Then discuss the questions that follow.

	The Adventurous Option		The Conservative Option	
1	A job that requires a lot of traveling		A job in one location	
2	An invigorationg walk on a cold day		Staying indoors on a cold day	
3	Meeting new people		Familiar old friends	
4	The freedom of single life		The safety and security of married life	
5	Experiences that are a little frightening		Pleasant experiences	
6	Driving fast and breaking traffic rules		Driving safely and obeying traffic laws	
7	Living life to the fullest		Finding peace and happiness	
8	A"plan-as-you-go"vacation		A well-planned, comfortable vacation	
9	Friends who are wild and unpredicatable		Friends who are calm and reliable	
10	An intriguing movie you've never heard of		A movie that got good reviews	
11	People who are emotionally expressive		People who are reserved	
12	Wearing whatever you feel like wearing		Wearing what is appropriate for the situation	
13	Vibrant colors and unusual patterns		Classic colors and patterns	
14	Music that is unique		Top 10 music	
	Total Score :		**Total Score :**	

1. After taking this short test, do you consider yourself an **adventurous** or a conservative person on the whole? Are you happy with this?
2. What are some of the pros and cons associated with being a reserved or safety-conscious person? What kinds of pros and cons are related to being an adventurous person?

3. Would you rather date a reserved person or an adventurous person? Why?
4. There are many people who are unlikely to try things that involve taking risks. What kinds of risks are you afraid of taking?
5. Have you ever learned something important from facing your fears and taking a risk? Describe the situation and explain what you learned from it?
6. What is the biggest risk you've ever taken?
7. Have you ever felt that you missed a golden opportunity only because you were reluctant try something new? Describe the situation.
8. Would you rather live a long, calm life or a short, exciting one?
9. Have you ever experienced 'serendipity'? Have you ever had a fortunate accident?
10. Sometimes things go disastrously, despite our most detailed planning. Has this ever happened to you?

Discussion

1. What do you think of people who are **thrill-seekers**? Do people who do extreme sports like skydiving or mountain climbing seem crazy to you, or do you understand why they do what they do?
2. If given the chance, would you be willing to try any of the extreme sports listed below? If you have already tried any of them, describe your experience.

hang gliding	parasailing	paragliding	scuba diving
bungee jumping	skydiving	shark diving	rock climbing
base jumping	white-water rafting	mountain biking	other

3. What's the most exciting or **adventurous** thing you've ever done? Describe your experience.
4. What do you think would have been the most exciting event in history to take part in?
5. Who is the most adventurous person you know? Why do you consider him or her adventurous?
6. Do you enjoy roller coasters? What is the scariest one you've ever been on? Have you ever ridden one that was too scary for you?
7. Do you think that **adrenaline** is addictive? Do you know anyone who is an "**adrenaline junky**"?
8. "There is risk involved in every single moment." Do you agree? Why or why not?
9. A lot of people like watching television to experience stimulating things **vicariously**. What is your favourite television program, and what about it interests you?
10. What country (other than your own) would you like to live in? Why? Describe what would be exciting and challenging about living there.

11. Some religions, like Buddhism and Christianity, teach that living a calm, routine life is an important key to finding lasting peace and happiness. What do you think they mean? Do you agree? If so, do you think that people who seek the momentary satisfaction of exciting experiences might be giving up long-term happiness?

12. Research indicates that our tendencies regarding **risk-taking** develop at a very young age. When you were young, did your parents encourage you to try new things or were you over-protected? Looking back, what do you think of your parents' attitude? How will you treat your own children?

13. Do you think that boys are encouraged to **take risks** more often than girls are? Do you think that this makes sense? Does it cause girls grow up to be too timid? Should this be changed?

14. How long do you think you could sit still and do absolutely nothing? What do you think this says about your personality?

15. In North America, children who are too out-going and adventurous are sometimes given a drug called 'Ritalin' to help them calm down so they can focus on things more intently. What do you think of this?

16. Do you think that the hectic pace of modern life causes us to **feel restless** and **crave excitement**?

17. Is your life interesting and full of many different experiences, or is it **tedious**, **monotonous** and **mundane**? Do you feel that you are **living life to the fullest**, or do you often feel that your life is following **a boring routine**? Is your daily routine making you feel **restless**?

18. Do you think that some people try to escape their boring life by **living vicariously through other people**? Do you know anyone who does this? Do parents sometimes **live vicariously through their children**? Do yours?

19. Do you know anyone who enjoys **living on the edge**, who loves the excitement that comes from taking risks?

LESSON

5 Crime Doesn't Pay

Language Points

to take your aggression / frustration out on someone / something
to take out your aggression / frustration on someone / something
I was angry and I took my frustration out on the photocopy machine. I punched it, kicked it and swore at it several times.

a serial killer
The most infamous serial killer in Canadian history confessed to killing 49 people.

law-abiding / a law-abiding citizen
Most people are law-abiding. They follow rules and don't break laws.

to crack down on something / a tough crackdown
The police have recently begun to crack down hard on drug dealers. I hope that the neighborhood becomes safer.

capital punishment / the death penalty
The serial murderer received capital punishment for his crimes.

to acquit / to be acquitted (of charges)
The lawyers were not able to prove that he was guilty, so he was acquitted of all charges. He is a free man.

to deter (crime) / to be deterred / a deterrent
Some people think that capital punishment deters violent crime, but others disagree.

an eye for an eye (a tooth for a tooth)
Some people believe in an eye for an eye: equal punishment or revenge.

to be executed / an execution
He was convicted of murder, and he is scheduled to be executed on July 30.

to get a sense of closure / to provide closure
The judge announced that the criminal would be spending the rest of his life in jail. For the victim, it was an emotionally satisfying end to a difficult experience. It provided him with a sense of closure.

Reading

The Mind of a Serial Killer

Most people believe they have control over their **impulses** and that no matter how angry they get, their conscience will stop them from **taking their aggression out on other people**. But what causes some people to completely lose control of themselves and commit murder - repeatedly? Do **serial killers** lack the sort of conscience that most of us **take for granted**?

For decades now, psychiatrists and FBI agents have tried to understand the mind of the serial killer - what causes these individuals to commit such **brutal** acts. Some of the causes they have uncovered in their studies include childhood abuse, genetics, chemical imbalances, brain injuries, and exposure to **traumatic** events. But none of these possible causes fully **accounts** for the terrible things that serial killers do.

Many murderers blame our culture. They claim that violence and sexuality in the media feeds their appetites. A few days before he was executed, the infamous Ted Bundy declared that pornography was responsible for his murderous **rampage**.

Other murderers are drawn to brutality as a way to escape their feelings of powerlessness and failure. The sense of completely **dominating** another human being makes them feel as though they aren't such a failure. This sense of power may **be fueled by** the coverage that their brutal acts receive in the media. They may feel that they are finally receiving the attention they deserve.

Still others may be attracted to the excitement of killing. They may see their lives as boring or **mundane**, and killing may be a way to break the **monotony**. "I wished I could stop but I couldn't; I had no other thrill or happiness," said serial killer Dennis Nilsen.

Regardless of their motivations, all serial killers live on the other side of our social boundaries. They represent the darkness, desire, and power that we must control within ourselves.

Comprehension

1. Do you know of any famous **serial killers** in your country? If so, can you remember any of the details of their crimes?

2. Can any of the reasons given in the article fully explain the brutal acts committed by serial killers or are such people simply evil?

3. The serial killer Ted Bundy blamed pornography for his crimes. To what extent do you think that media sex and violence are responsible for violent crime?

4. The article suggests that the news coverage given to serial killers only encourages them. Do you agree? If so, does the media have a responsibility not to sensationalize such events, or perhaps not even to cover them?

5. What do you think is an appropriate punishment for serial killers?

6. Do you think that there is ever any justification for murder? Explain your answer.

7. At some point in our lives, we may feel an urge to seriously harm or even kill someone who makes us very angry. What is it that stops us? Is it our conscience, fear of punishment, social upbringing or something else?

Dialogue

A man is being interrogated by an investigator.

Arnold: I already told you that it wasn't me. I don't know who did it, but it sure wasn't me! I've always been a **law-abiding** citizen. I wouldn't hurt a fly.

Officer: Then, where were you on Saturday afternoon at around 4?

Arnold: I was at the movies, I **swear**!

Officer: Do you have an **alibi**?

Arnold: Yeah, sure, my wife! We saw the new James Bond movie. It was the 2:30 matinee. She'd **vouch for** me.

Officer: We'll check that out later. Arthur Collins was your brother-in-law. And we have **eye-witnesses** that are willing to **testify** that they saw the two of you having a **heated** argument in the parking lot of a donut shop a few hours before he was murdered. That makes you our main **suspect**. Is it true? Did you or didn't you have an argument with Mr. Collins shortly before he was murdered?

Arnold: Yeah, sure; Art and I had our differences, but I wouldn't have killed him. We were just talking about how he didn't clean my golf clubs after he borrowed them. It wasn't anything serious. I didn't kill him, that's for sure. I was at the movies, for crying out loud!

Officer: Alright, but I'm sure that you'll be curious to know that the new James Bond movie stopped playing on Friday. So, do you want to **reconsider** your story?

Arnold: Uh...uh...er...I don't want to answer any more questions until my lawyer gets here.

Officer: Hmm. That's the most intelligent thing you've said all afternoon.

Comprehension

1. Do you feel that the police do a good job of **enforcing laws**? Justify your opinion.

2. Do most people have respect for the law and the police? Support your opinion with examples.

3. Do you find the police intimidating? Would you ever approach a police officer to ask for help, directions, etc.?

4. Have you ever **witnessed a crime**? What happened? Have you ever been asked to give evidence or testimony?

5. Do you think that there is such a thing as a '**perfect crime**'? Or is there always some way for the police to find out who did it?

6. When the police arrest someone, what rights, if any, do you think the accused should have?

7. Should the police be allowed to use coercion, physical force, threats, or psychological intimidation to get information or confessions from suspects? What sort of 'techniques' should be permissible and which should not?

8. Are there any laws in your country that you think need to be changed?

9. What are some of the things police have been '**cracking down on**' recently?

10. Have police in your country been susceptible to **bribery**? Is this still a problem?

Activity A

Crime and Punishment

From the list on the right, select the most appropriate punishment for the crimes listed on the left. Explain why you think the punishment fits the crime.

Crime

- **Treason** (crimes against your country)
- **1st Degree Murder** (murder planned in advance)
- **2nd Degree Murder** (unplanned murder)
- **Manslaughter** (killing in self-defense)
- **Kidnapping** (taking and keeping someone prisoner, to exchange for something)
- **Armed Robbery** (stealing while using weapons as a threat)
- **Robbery / Mugging** (stealing someone's belongings)
- **Sexual Assault** (sexual crimes)
- **Arson** (setting fire to property)
- **Embezzlement / Fraud** (taking money from a company)
- **Drug possession / Drug Trafficking**
- **Drunk Driving**
- **Physical Assault** (physical attack)
- **Theft**
- **Shoplifting** (stealing goods from a shop)
- **Damage to Property / Vandalism**

Punishment

- **Capital Punishment** (the death penalty)
- **Corporal Punishment** (hitting or beating)
- **Life Imprisonment**
- **5- or 10-year Prison Term**
- **Home Detention** (the offender is not allowed to leave their house)
- **Loss of Driving Privileges**
- **Fine**
- **Restitution** (the offender must re-pay someone for the damage or loss they have caused them)
- **Community Service** (the offender must work around their community to pay for their crime)
- **Probation** (a period of time during which a criminal has to obey the law and be supervised by a probation officer instead of going to prison)

Activity B

You Be the Judge

Consider the following situations with your classmate(s). What do you think is an appropriate punishment in each case? Try to be as specific as possible. For example, if you think someone should receive a fine, how much should it be? If you think someone should go to prison, how long should his or her sentence be? If you think that someone is not guilty, you can acquit them of all charges.

1 It is 4 a.m. and Steven is having a loud argument with his girlfriend Sue. He continues banging on the door and shouting for several minutes, waking all neighbors, one of whom calls the police. Two of Sue's windows are broken and her door is damaged. The couple has a history of violence.

2 Three foreigners are caught by customs officers trying to enter your home country with drugs hidden in their suitcases. They say the drugs are for personal use, not for sale.

3 After pushing in front of a pregnant woman to get a seat on a crowded subway train, a drunken middle-aged man gets into a fight with a young guy who criticizes him. The drunkard gets a good beating from the younger, stronger man and ends up in hospital for 20 days.

4 Jason is caught **pick-pocketing** in a busy department store by a security guard. He is 18 years old and is part of a gang who are well known by the police for troublemaking.

5 A man is late for an important meeting at work. If he doesn't get there on time, he will lose an important client. He gets pulled over by the police for speeding and running a red light.

6 Michael was jaywalking on his way home after an evenings drinking. He was hit by car and his leg was broken. After the car sped away without stopping, Brian got the license number.

7 A pervert is arrested for flashing some female students outside their high school.

Activity C

Debate: Capital Punishment

You will be asked to defend one of the following positions. Before you begin, read over the supporting arguments and decide which one(s) you will focus on. Also consider some of the questions listed below. During the debate, remember to listen carefully to opposing positions and respond to their points

POSITION ONE We should have the death penalty	POSITION TWO We shouldn't have the death penalty
• Some crimes are so brutal that the criminals who committed them deserve **the death penalty**. People who take another human life should forfeit their own lives.	• Killing is immoral. It is always wrong – even if the criminal is guilty of a brutal crime. We should respect life – even the life of a convicted killer.
• Taxpayers should not have to pay money to keep the most violent criminals in prison.	• No price can be put on a human life.
• **Capital punishment** deters murder. Society should use the strongest punishment available to **deter** murder – and the strongest punishment is the death penalty.	• Murders still happen in countries that have the death penalty. Criminals never expect to get caught, so they **are not deterred by** capital punishment.
• **Wrongful executions** happen sometimes, but they are very rare.	• Judges and juries sometimes make mistakes. Innocent people are sometimes convicted and executed.
• The death penalty gives society a strong message that killing is unacceptable.	• The **death penalty** encourages violent crime because it condones killing and gives the message that killing is acceptable. It desensitizes society to killing.
• The death penalty **provides a sense of closure** for the victims' family.	• Society's broader interests are more important than giving victims' families **a sense of closure**.
• Life in prison is too lenient as a punishment. Life in prison means watching TV, reading and chatting.	• Life in prison is an appropriate sentence.

Some questions to think about:

1. Does your country have capital punishment? Has your country abolished it? If so, when was it abolished? When was the last execution? Why was it abolished?

2. Do you agree with capital punishment? In what cases is it justified? Can you think of any recent cases in your country where you feel the criminal deserved execution?

3. What do you think of the argument "**an eye for an eye, a tooth for a tooth**" – a life for a life?

4. Does the death penalty **deter** violent crime?

5. Do you think victims' families **get a sense of closure** knowing a killer has been executed?

6. What is the best alternative to the death penalty? Life imprisonment?

6. Does the death penalty desensitize us to killing?

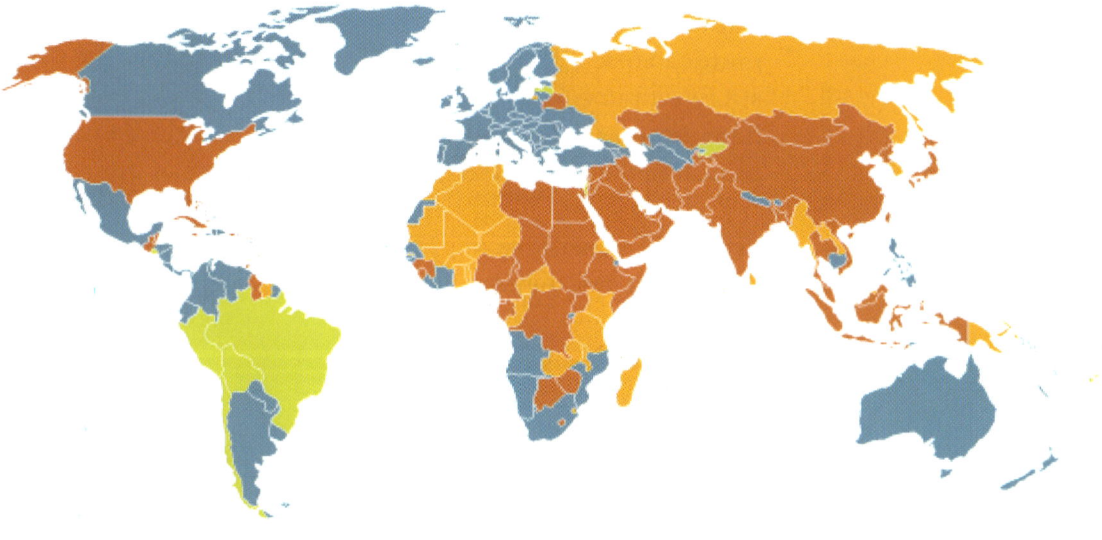

Use of the death penalty around the world (September 2007)

- Abolished for all offenses (92 countries)
- Abolished for all offenses except under special circumstances (10 countries)
- Retains, though not used for at least 10 years (32 countries)
- Retains death penalty (64 countries)

Discussion

1. When you are angry or frustrated, do you sometimes **take out your frustrations on something**? Do you ever bang your fist on the table, kick a food or drink machine, punch the printer, etc? Have you ever regretted **taking out your frustrations on someone**?
2. Are there any infamous **serial killers** in your country? Have they been caught? How many people did they kill? Did they deny their crimes, or did they confess? What punishment did they receive? Was the punishment appropriate? Too severe? Too lenient?
3. Are there any laws in your country that should be **enforced** more strictly? Why are they not **enforced** more strictly at present? Should the police **crackdown on** any illegal activities?
4. Are there some illegal activities in your country that you think should **be legalized**?
5. Are some parts of your home city considered more dangerous than others? Which parts? What are the main causes of crime in the dangerous areas? Are there any places you are afraid to visit because of the high crime rate? If so, what places?
6. Do you think that your home country is a safe place to live? Which countries is it safer than, and which countries is it less safe than? Explain.
7. Are you **apprehensive** about walking outside after dark? Why or why not?
8. Do you always lock your house? How about your car? Why or why not?
9. Have you ever had **a break-in** at your home? Do you know anyone who has been **mugged** or **robbed**? What happened?
10. Have you ever been **pick pocketed**? What happened?
11. Do you think people who use illegal drugs should be put in jail? Why or why not?
12. Do you think there are any legal drugs that should be illegal (or **vice versa**)?
13. Do you think that **capital punishment** is a good idea? Why or why not?
14. What crimes deserve **the death penalty**? Explain your opinion.
15. Does imprisonment rehabilitate sex offenders? What treatment programs do you think would cure **child molesters**?
16. Do you think that punishment for violent crimes should be the same for **juveniles (minors)** and adults? Why or why not?
17. When should a juvenile or minor be **tried** as an adult?
18. Does prison help **rehabilitate** criminals? Or does prison just **harden** criminals? Is prison an effective punishment? Why or why not?
19. What do you think a typical day is like for a prisoner?
20. Does crime pay? Is some crime worth the risk of punishment?
21. Have you ever **witnessed** a crime? Describe what happened.

22. Is it ever okay to break the law? If so, when? In which situations would you commit a crime?

23. What do you think is the worst crime? Why?

24. What makes some people become criminals? Is it poverty, **upbringing**, lack of education, unemployment, society or something else?

25. What would you do if you heard a **burglar** in your house?

26. Do you trust the police? Do the police do a good job of **enforcing** the law? Justify your opinion.

27. Do you think that movies and the news media **glorify** criminal behaviour? Why?

28. Do you enjoy **gangster movies**? Why?

29. Can you think of any high-profile cases in your country in which someone was accused of a crime, but then acquitted? What crime were they accused of? Why were they **acquitted**? Was there not enough evidence?

LESSON

6 Us and Them

Language Points

to discriminate against someone / discrimination
Our manager discriminates against my friend Chen, just because he's Chinese. Everyone in our department has gotten a raise, except him.

racism / a racist
I get really upset whenever I hear someone make a racist comment about Chinese people.

stereotype
There are all sorts of stupid stereotypes that people have about the Chinese. Some people think all Chinese are dishonest or smelly.

prejudice
When Chinese people emigrate to Western countries they often have to deal with a lot of prejudice, injustice and mistreatment.

misconception
But these stereotypes - that they are dishonest or smelly or whatever - are inaccurate. They are misconceptions.

ethnic / ethnicity
I don't think that a person's ethnicity has anything to do with their value or worth as a person.

multicultural
Western countries are all multicultural, so I don't understand why these stereotypes still persist.

cultural diversity
Personally, I think that cultural diversity is what makes Canada an interesting place to live. You can meet all sorts of people here.

Dialogue

A man gets into a taxi.

Boris: Where to?
Jason: Hmm. I'm not sure actually. I just got here, and I wanted to do some sightseeing. What would you recommend?
Boris: What kind of things are you interested in?
Jason: Well, I like art. I've heard that the Walsh Museum is quite good. Do you know anything about it?
Boris: Oh, you don't want to go there. That's in the gay neighborhood. There are lots of **homos** walking around holding hands and kissing and stuff. I'd stay away from there if I were you.
Jason: Hmm. Well, that's alright. Why don't you take me there?
Boris: Suit yourself.
Jason: What's the big deal? What's wrong with gay people?

Boris: Oh, you know. They're sick **perverts**. They're not normal. And a lot of them have AIDS. You don't want some **queer** bumping into you on the street. You might catch it.

Jason: Hmm. I know quite a few gay people, and they're not 'sick' at all. In fact, they're quite nice. What makes you think they're 'sick'? I'll bet you've probably never even talked to a gay person before. Have you?

Boris: Talk to one? If I met one, I'd probably punch him in the face. It makes me sick to my stomach to even think about those...

Jason: What did gay people ever do to you?

Boris: Nothing. It's just that they're so...

Jason: Look. I wasn't going to get into this, but now you're going too far. I can't tell you who you should like. But you should really give people a chance before you judge them as this or that. And I don't think anyone deserves to be punched in the face just because they're gay.

Boris: Why the hell should you care?

Jason: Well... because I'm gay, that's why.

Boris: Uhh....

Jason: Could you let me off here, please? I think I'd rather take the subway.

Comprehension

1. In the dialogue, Boris is making **stereotypes** about gay people. Do you also have a tendency to stereotype certain categories of people that you've never met?
2. Is it ever acceptable to stereotype, or should we judge everyone individually? When might it be permissible to stereotype others?
3. What reasons do people usually give for disliking gay people? Do you agree with any of these? If so, which ones?
4. What do you think of the way Jason handled this situation?
5. Would you react similarly to Jason if someone made negative comments about your religion, ethnicity, etc? Or would you try to avoid confrontation? Why?
6. How would you describe people's attitudes toward homosexuality in your country? Do you think people's attitudes have changed during the last ten years? If so, have attitudes become more liberal and tolerant?
7. Why do you think that negative stereotyping is more common than positive stereotyping?
8. Do you think that a person's negative stereotypes about various groups tend to disappear once they have gotten to know a few people from that group? Why do you think this might be?

Activity A

Tell the Truth!

Every society has groups of people about whom there are stereotypes: housewives, politicians, immigrants, and people from the country are examples. Sometimes the stereotypes are positive and sometimes they are negative. With your classmate(s), talk about the stereotypes that people in your country have associated with the different social groups listed below.

- Men
- Women
- Doctors
- Politicians
- Lawyers
- Auto mechanics
- Homosexuals
- Americans
- The British
- Southeast Asians
- The Chinese
- Black people
- White people
- The rich
- The Japanese
- Teenagers
- The elderly
- Movie stars

Then discuss the following questions.

1. Where do you think these stereotypes come from?
2. To what extent do you think they are true?
3. Do you think that some of them should be changed? In what ways?
4. What effects do you think these stereotypes have?

Activity B

What Would You Do?

Read the following situations and talk with your classmate(s) about what you would do.

1 Imagine that you are visiting another country, and you've just checked into a hotel. As you're getting off the elevator to go to your room, some of the people still on the elevator laugh and say something that sounds insulting. The elevator door hasn't closed yet. What would you do?

2 Imagine that there is a woman who was recently hired at your company. She's been working there for three weeks now and has been complaining that your boss keeps asking her to make coffee for him and his business associates. The problem is that making coffee isn't part of her job description, so she's understandably upset. What would you do?

3 You and your very good-looking friend knowingly apply for the same job at the same company. Although you did better in school and have a more impressive resume, your friend gets hired instead of you. How would you feel? What would you do?

4 Imagine that you get on the subway after a very long day at work to find that the only seat available is next to some homeless men. What would you do?

5 Imagine that you check the computer to see what websites your son has been visiting, and you find that he has visited many holocaust-denial websites. What would you do? Why?

6 Your teacher pays attention only to the prettiest girl / most handsome guy in the class. You notice this during the first week, but it keeps happening well into the month. What would you do?

7 You ask your male friend if he is ever going to get a girlfriend. Then he shocks you by telling you that he is gay. He wants to introduce you to his boyfriend. What would you say, and how would you react?

Activity C

Discrimination Elimination

You and your partner have been appointed by the government to help eliminate all forms of discrimination in your country. Discuss examples of each kind of discrimination and your solutions to eliminate them. Write notes in the appropriate columns below. Then be prepared to report your suggestions to the class.

	Examples	Your solutions
Discrimination based on race (including skin color, country of origin, etc.)		
Discrimination based on gender		
Discrimination based on age		
Discrimination based on maritial status		
Discrimination based on appearance (including height, weight, body build, etc.)		
Discrimination based on economic/social class		

Discussion

1. If you've studied or traveled abroad, were you ever a victim of racism? Have you ever been discriminated against? What happened?
2. Are mixed marriages becoming more common in your country? Do many people in your country **have prejudices against** mixed marriages?
3. Is there a lot of cronyism (favoritism towards friends) and nepotism (favoritism towards family members) in business and politics in your home country? Is it reasonable for people to give preferential treatment to friends and family, in hiring situations, for example? Or is this a form of prejudice?
4. What are some **stereotypes** that people in your country have about foreigners living here? Are these stereotypes fair, or are they **misconceptions**?
5. Do you have any prejudices?
6. If you thought your son was gay or your daughter a lesbian, how would you feel? What would you do?

7. In your opinion, are **multiculturalism** and **cultural diversity** good for a country? Would you like to see your country become more **multicultural** and **culturally diverse**?

8. Have you ever **been discriminated against**? Because of your race? Because of your sex?

9. Do you see any evidence of **racism** in your country? Are certain ethnic or **racial groups discriminated against**? If so, give some examples. If not, why do you think there is no racism?

10. Are there many third-world migrant workers in your country? Do they face any **discrimination**?

11. Have you ever made a **racist** joke? How did you feel after making it? Did anyone seem offended by it?

12. Have you ever heard anyone make a **racist** joke? How did you feel / react?

13. It has been said that everyone's a little bit **racist**. Are all people racists in some ways? What makes you think so?

14. Which **ethnic** groups do you feel the least comfortable around? Which ethnic groups do you feel the most comfortable around? Why?

15. What do you think about Hollywood's **depictions** of blacks? Of Asians? Of Arabs?

16. What are some **common misconceptions** that foreigners have about people from your country?

17. Are there any countries that don't suffer from **racial conflict**? Which countries have the most extreme **racial tensions**?

18. Do you feel uncomfortable even talking about racism? Why?

19. How can we end racism?

20. Is regionalism important in your country? Are some regions favored at the expense of other regions? Is regionalism important in politics in your country?

21. Is racism more prevalent in some countries than others?

LESSON

7 Take Your Pick

Language Points

to beat around the bush

Stop beating around the bush and tell me what you really think.

to settle on a decision / to be settled / to make up (one's) mind (to do something)

I've settled on a decision. I'm going to take a year off university to concentrate on making music. I've been thinking about it a lot, and I've made up my mind.

to foresee (all) the implications of a decision

The implications of a big decision are not always clear when you make the decision. You often can't foresee all the things that happen because of the decision.

to rule out a choice / to rule something out

We ruled out going to New York for a vacation because it was going to be too expensive.

a priority / priorities / to prioritize

You have to learn to prioritize. And getting a good job should be your top priority.

to weigh different options

Some people like to weigh the different options before they make a decision. They think about the pros and cons of each choice.

to follow your gut / instincts / gut instincts

Some people follow their gut instincts. They make decisions based on their feelings and don't spend a lot of time analyzing things logically.

to turn to someone (for help, advice, etc.)

When I have a big problem, I usually turn to my best friends or parents for advice.

to strike / find a balance (between two things) / to balance something and something else

I want to strike a balance between my career and my family.

to exert (an) influence (on / over something / someone)

A powerful mother exerts a lot of influence over her children.

Dialogue

Two newlyweds are discussing their future together.

Fred: Hey, Cath. Do you have a sec? Why don't we sit down and talk about some stuff?

Cathy: Uh...alright. What...sort of stuff?

Fred: Mmm...I've been thinking for a while about something, and I just wanted to see what you thought about it.

Cathy: So, what is it?! You don't have to **beat around the bush**!

Fred: Alright, alright. Well, we've got a bit of money saved up, and my career is going well. I'm making enough to support the two of us...

Cathy: Yeah. Where are you going with this?

Fred: Well, I know we've talked about having kids in a few years, but I don't want to wait too long. You know, we're not getting any younger, Cath.

Cathy: Listen, I thought **it was all settled**. You know I value my career more than anything else. We've already made a firm decision to wait before we have children. I don't understand why you're suddenly changing your mind.

Fred: It's just that all of our friends are having babies, and I feel like we're falling behind. I guess I thought that you weren't really that serious about your career, but I guess you are.

Cathy: I've got an idea, Fred. Why don't you take one or two years off from your career to raise the baby? You know, like Mr. Mom. Then I have absolutely no problem with starting a family right now.

Fred: Oh, well, if you put it that way, maybe we could wait a few more years.

Comprehension

1. Is it always fair to expect a woman to give up her career to start a family? Explain why you think so.

2. Do you think Cathy and Fred's situation is common among couples in your country?

3. If a wife were making more money than her husband, should she keep her job and get her husband to stay home and raise their children?

4. Lately, more and more couples have been opting to delay having children until after establishing their careers. What do you think are the pros and cons of having children when you are older?

5. People are having fewer children, compared to thirty or forty years ago. How can you explain this trend?

6. What do you think of Cathy's choices?

7. When you **make up your mind to do something**, are you usually stubborn or are you willing to compromise with others?

Reading

There are certain decisions that we all have to make in life that seem to be more important than others. Perhaps it is because they have a significant **impact** on the course that our life will take. We choose the university that we want to attend. We choose our major. We choose who we will date. We choose who we will marry. We choose the house that we will buy. These are the sorts of decisions that cause our life to **veer off** in one direction or another.

But making these sorts of decisions is not always easy because it usually involves a lot of uncertainty. It is almost impossible for us to know which options will work out best for us in the long term. With all of life's twists and turns, it is impossible to **foresee all of the implications** of a decision. With the **myriad** of factors that are involved, it is impossible to take everything into account. Some people find **reassurance** in the knowledge that greater forces - either God or Fate - are guiding their life in the right direction. For others, the issue is more complicated.

The other aspect of making life decisions that **poses a challenge** is the sacrifices, both obvious and **obscure**, that one must make. Whenever we choose to follow one course of action, it **entails** that we are unable to follow another. For example, if you decide to return to school to further your education, you will be giving up the **seniority** and work-experience that you could otherwise gain on the job, not to mention the money. Of course, there may also be benefits, but making choices almost always **goes hand in hand with** making sacrifices.

Sometimes the choices that we make mean that future choices are **ruled out** or at least limited. If you decided to study medicine in university, and then started your career as a doctor only to discover that it did not really appeal to you, it might be quite difficult, although not impossible, to be retrained for another field. At the very least, it would have been an expensive and time-consuming mistake.

Given all of these **mind-boggling** aspects of decision-making, it is a wonder that we ever make any decisions at all! Perhaps our decisions are, to some extent, modeled on the decisions of the people that we admire or the image of who we want to be. When we look at decisions that others have made and how things have turned out for them, it may be easier to see the likely results of the choices that face us in our own lives.

Comprehension

1. Do you think that decision-making nowadays is becoming more complex and stressful? Give some examples of situations in which you feel burdened with too many choices.

2. What are some of the reasons that making decisions is difficult, according to the article?

3. Do you tend to make decisions impulsively, or do you take some time to think about the future implications first?

4. Can you remember a decision that seemed unimportant at the time but later ended up having a life-changing effect?

5. Do you tend to put off making difficult decisions until the last minute?

6. Some people say that there is no such thing as a wrong decision if you consider the experience that results from each decision as being beneficial in some way. To what extent do you agree with this statement?

7. Have you ever made an important decision that at first seemed to be wrong, but eventually turned out to be for the best? What happened?

8. To what extent do you let other people influence your decision-making?

9. Do you consider yourself good at making difficult decisions in stressful situations?

10. What, according to the article, makes decision-making more manageable? Do you have any of your own strategies to help you make difficult decisions?

Activity A

Milestones

Although everyone's life is unique, there are certain transitions that most of us make over the course of our lives. Look at the timeline below and discuss the questions that follow with your classmate(s).

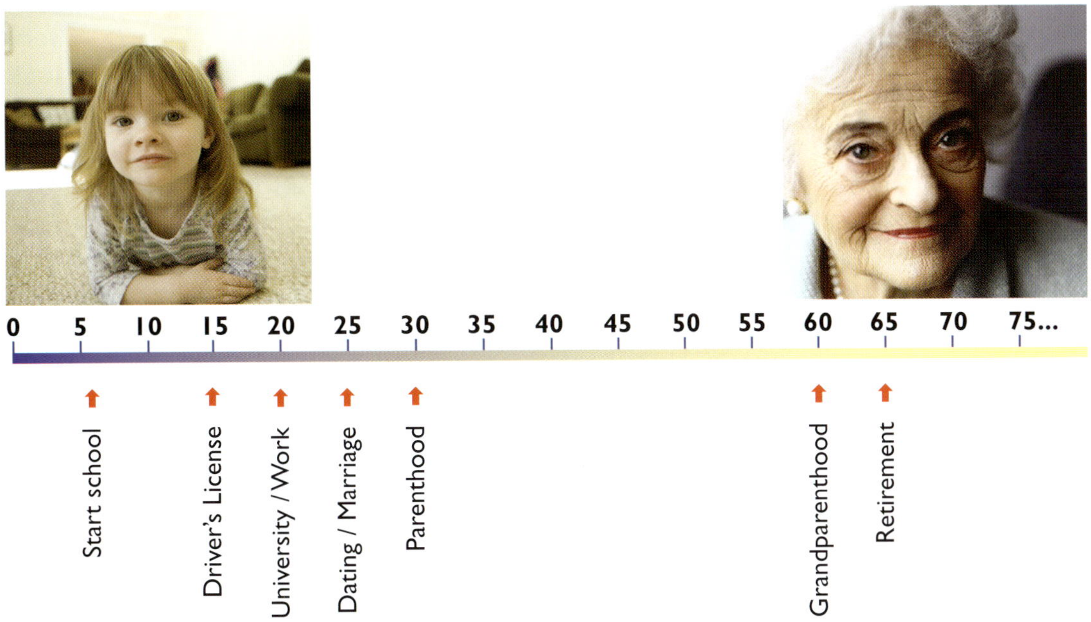

1. Does this timeline match your life (as how you anticipate it unfolding)? If not, how does it differ?
2. At what age did you / do you think you will; start working, get married, have a child, retire?
3. How do you think people's priorities change at each of the milestones listed above?
4. What other significant 'milestones' can you think of? Why are they significant?
5. In some cultures, there are rites of passage that mark people's transition from childhood into adulthood. What marks this transition in your country? When should people be considered adults?
6. What are some of the challenges that people face in their twenties, thirties, forties, etc.? What are some of the opportunities each period offers?
7. What have been the best and worst years of your life so far? Why? Be specific.
8. Describe one memorable event from each of the stages of life (e.g., your teens, your college life, your late twenties, etc.) that you have already passed through.
9. Some people say that learning is a lifelong journey. What important lessons do you think you've learned in your life so far?
10. Some people never seem to fully mature. Even though they are adults, they act like children. What do you think separates adults from children?

Activity B

The Key to Success

How would you define a successful life? Think about people you admire. With your classmate(s) discuss which of the following you consider key elements in a successful life. Explain why.

- love
- self-esteem
- integrity
- openness
- forgiveness
- patience
- flexibility
- responsibility
- courage
- honesty
- life-experience
- imagination
- independence
- education
- accomplishment
- wealth
- sense of humor
- luck
- religious beliefs
- diligence
- loyalty
- foresight
- trust
- family values

Activity C

The Road Less Traveled

Read about the choices the following people made, and then discuss the questions that follow with your classmate(s).

Max Bingham

Max dropped out of high school early because he never enjoyed studying. Instead, because of his love of computers, he spent all his time learning computer languages. Eventually, he became a freelancer for several large software companies where his expertise became highly valuable. He has a good reputation and decides his own hours and salary. He is not in a relationship.

Zeke Reinforth

Zeke graduated with a degree in Engineering. He landed a good job at a major semiconductor conglomerate. Although he has enjoyed his work there over the last 10 years, working alone in a lab makes it difficult to get to know his co-workers. He makes a decent salary but cannot easily afford the luxuries he desires. He is not married.

Naomi Left

Naomi studied Psychology in college. Before meeting and falling in love with her husband-to-be, she worked with patients at a mental hospital for 5 years. Soon after marriage, she got pregnant with their first child and had to quit her job to raise her family. Although she loves her children and her husband, she often feels dissatisfied with her lifestyle and lack of challenges.

Derek Zanfitz

Derek majored in Business Administration but couldn't find a job. Instead, he applied for social welfare and started selling marijuana to make some extra money. He soon discovered that he could make more money doing this than most of his friends could make at their 'legitimate' jobs. Sometimes, he likes to smoke it with his friends and often spends his money traveling to other countries. People who know him describe his life as 'one long holiday'. Although he is not married, he says this is not a priority for him.

Carrie McNeil

Carrie is a devout Catholic. Because she has decided to become a nun, she cannot marry and must remain celibate for the rest of her life. She does not care about wealth, fashion or having children, as she trusts fully in her choice to serve God. Despite what many people think, she claims to be truly happy.

Follow-up Discussion

1. Which of these people do you envy? Who would you least want to be like?
2. Which one can you relate to most? In which ways are you similar to that person?
3. Overall, who do you think seems most content with their life?
4. Who's life would you criticize the most and why? If you were that person, what would you have done differently?
5. If these people were from your country, how would they fit into mainstream society?
6. Who do you think has the hardest life? Do you think that your life is hard right now? Do you think that it is likely to get harder in the future?
7. In the future, which of these people do you think is most likely to regret the choices they have made? So far in your life, which choices do you most regret and why?
8. Give a brief outline of your life story.

Discussion

1. What are your **priorities** in life? Are there some things that you have had to sacrifice because of your **priorities**?
2. Are there any choices you've made in your life that you regret? Why? If you had a second chance, what would you do differently?
3. Have you ever made a decision in order to make someone else happy? Who?
4. Do you think that getting married makes the future decision-making process more or less complicated? Is it easier being able to share the burden of decision-making with someone else, or does it become harder to reach an agreement? Explain your answer.

5. When we are young, most of us try to imagine what life will be like for us when we grow up. To what extent does your present life resemble your childhood expectations?

6. These days, are you finding it difficult to **strike a balance between** different aspects of your life such as work responsibilities and family? If so, which ones?

7. Do you often take other people's advice about what to do in your life, or do you usually prefer to make decisions on your own?

8. Have you **settled on an important decision** recently? What did you decide? Why?

9. Are you good at **prioritizing**? What are your top priorities at present? Are your priorities the same as your friends'?

10. Do men and women usually have similar or different **priorities**?

11. Do you find it easy or difficult to make decisions? Why?

12. How do you make decisions? Do you think about them for a long time, **weighing the different options**? Or do you **follow your gut instincts**?

13. Can you think of some decisions that you've made that have had a particularly significant impact on how your life unfolded? How do you think your life would have been different if you had chosen differently?

14. Is there anyone who you consider a role model? How have they influenced you? Do you think that some of your important decisions have been influenced by your role model(s)?

15. How much do you think that our adult choices are affected by our childhood upbringing?

16. To what extent do you feel that external forces such as God or fate control your life?

17. When you have a really difficult and important decision to make, who do you usually **turn to for help**; your parents, a trusted friend, a fortune-teller, or someone else?

18. Do you ever get a '**gut feeling**' that you should make a particular decision, even when that decision seems to be wrong? Do decisions that you make based on your 'gut feelings' usually turn out well?

19. In some countries, parents generally believe in allowing children to make all of their own decisions. In other countries, parents feel that they have the right to **exert an influence** in their adult children's lives, even if the children are in their 30s. What is the situation in your country?

20. Have you ever made a big decision, but failed to **foresee all the implications of the decision**? What decision did you make? And what were the **unforeseen implications**?

21. Do you have a lot of **foresight**? Do you have any friends or relatives who have the **foresight** to always seem to be making good decisions?

LESSON

8 Aging Gracefully

Language Points

to age gracefully

He is aging so gracefully. He looks younger than his age, and he is so energetic.

to be full of life and vigor

Teenagers are full of life and vigor.

spry

The old gentleman is as spry as he had been when he was much younger. He is still lively and active.

to be prone to (something) / to become increasingly prone to (something)

I worry that I am prone to cancer because many of my relatives have died from the disease. That's why I get a medical check-up every six months.

to pass away

My grandfather passed away in 2001. He was 83 years old.

to live to be a ripe old age / to live to the ripe old age of

My grandmother lived to the ripe old age of 96.

a nursing home

People who cannot take care of themselves anymore sometimes move into a nursing home, a kind of private hospital for the elderly.

to be cared for

When some people become old they can no longer take care of themselves, so they have to be cared for. They are often cared for by a private nurse or relatives.

to be out of touch

My grandparents often offer me advice, but they are so out of touch. They don't understand the realities of the modern world.

to go senile

It is very upsetting to see somebody go senile. They become confused, forget things easily, and can't take care of themselves very well.

longevity

Longevity often runs in families. If your parents and grandparents lived long lives, you can also expect to live for a long time.

Reading

We often get **contradictory** impressions about what it means to grow old in modern society. On one hand, medical technology and advances in research into **the aging process** promise to extend the human life-span significantly beyond what it is currently. But, on the other hand, we **face the prospect** of a life **confined to a nursing home** full of elderly people who feel **superfluous**. Modern medicine will allow us to live longer, but will this be a curse or a blessing?

As more and more of us are destined to live into our eighties, we are challenged to plan for our old age sooner in life to ensure that we age gracefully and comfortably. Occasionally, we meet great-grandparents who are **full of life and**

vigor and we wonder what we can do to live to be as old and as healthy as they are. What combination of factors come together to help someone live to be a **spry centenarian**?

Of course, clear answers are not possible - at least not yet. However, there are studies underway that offer us a **tantalizing glimpse** at the secrets of aging well.

The Harvard Study of Adult Development has been following the lives of 864 individuals, selected as teenagers, for over 60 years. It offers information about what successful aging is and how it can be achieved. Among the many significant findings to **emerge** from the study thus far are the following:

- A happy marriage at age 50 was a reliable **predictor** of positive aging at 80. But surprisingly, low **cholesterol** levels at age 50 were not.
- The more close relationships test subjects maintained into their senior years, the better they were able to deal with the stresses related to loss and tragedy.
- Alcohol abuse always predicted unsuccessful aging, in part because alcoholism damaged future social supports.
- Developing new interests after retirement, and finding younger friends as older ones are lost, contributes more to life's enjoyment than retirement income.
- Objective good physical health was less important to successful aging than attitude towards one's health.

In general, the Harvard study would seem to suggest that a positive attitude and the support of friends contribute more to the quality of life in our senior years than any other factors. Of course, maintaining a healthy lifestyle, eating properly, and getting enough exercise can't hurt. But, if the findings of this study are to be believed, we would be wise to focus on our social and psychological well-being, in addition to our financial and physical health.

Comprehension

1. How would you summarize the findings of the Harvard study? What do these findings mean to you?

2. Does reading this article make you think differently about getting old?

3. How long do you want to live? If you could ensure that your quality of life would not significantly worsen, would you want to live to be 120 years old? Why or why not?

4. As people grow older, they **become increasingly prone to** loneliness and depression. What will you do to stay socially active after retirement?

5. Are there any people you know over 80 who seem to be **in remarkably good health**? What do you figure their secret is?

6. This article refers to the value of maintaining hobbies or interests after retirement. What sorts of hobbies or interests are appropriate for people over the age of 70? If their health is still relatively good, what sorts of activities do you think would offer the elderly the most enjoyment?

Activity A

Activity - Give It Up

The process of growing older usually entails gradually giving up the things that we have taken for granted throughout our lives. With your classmate(s), look at the list below and discuss the questions that follow.

- ☐ Chewing meat
- ☐ Driving
- ☐ Being thin
- ☐ Having teeth
- ☐ Remembering things
- ☐ Dressing fashionably
- ☐ Social graces / manners
- ☐ Having wrinkle-free skin
- ☐ Going to the nightclub
- ☐ Walking quickly
- ☐ Hearing what people are saying to you
- ☐ Being physically strong
- ☐ Reading normal-size print
- ☐ Having a lot of hair

1. Which of the items in the list will be the hardest for you to give up?
2. At what age do you expect to have to give it up?
3. How will you manage without it?
4. Which item will be the easiest to give up?

Vocabulary Focus

Fill in the blanks in the sentences using the appropriate expressions from the list.

- pass away
- spry
- the ripe old age of
- be out of touch
- be prone to
- have a stroke
- longevity
- go senile

1. I think I'm ________________ because I keep forgetting things.
2. He's not as __________ as he used to be. He's having trouble getting around these days
3. After he ____________, his left side was paralyzed.
4. The whole family was saddened by the news that their beloved grandmother ________ yesterday.
5. I recently read an article in the newspaper about a man from England, Buster Martin, who ran a full marathon at _______________ of 101.
6. He avoids foods that are high in cholesterol because his doctor warned him that he _______________ heart disease.
7. My 95-year-old great aunt attributes her _______________ to her positive attitude and healthy diet.
8. Some older people _______________ with younger folks, but others try hard to understand young people and their concerns.

Activity B

Care Options for Aging Parents

The good news is that our parents are more likely to **live to be a ripe old age**. The bad news is that somehow they will have to be cared for. As our parents age, they undergo an inevitable process of becoming increasingly reliant on others. This may happen gradually, or suddenly if they are stricken with serious medical problems. At some point, the decision will have to be made about how they will be best cared for.

With your classmate(s), discuss the pros and cons of the various options listed below. Use the questions that follow as a guide for your discussion.

Living on their own with minimal assistance
Living with the family
Living in a retirement community
Living in a nursing home
Other

Consider the following:

- availability of regular medical care
- proximity to emergency medical treatment
- proximity to family members
- opportunities for social interaction
- independence and mobility required
- cost

Activity C

Aging and Growing Older: Famous Sayings

Do you know any famous sayings or idioms in your native language about aging and growing older? Share the sayings with the class. Then, with your partner, read the quotations below about aging and growing older and discuss the meaning of each quote. Which ones do you like best? Do you agree or disagree with them?

1. The last birthday that's any good is 23. - *Andy Rooney*
2. How old would you be if you didn't know how old you was? - *Satchel Paige*
3. A man is not old until his regrets take the place of dreams. - *John Barrymore*
4. Men do not quit playing because they grow old; they grow old because they quit playing. - *Oliver Wendell Holmes*
5. Nature gives you the face you have at twenty; it is up to you to merit the face you have at fifty. - *Coco Chanel*

6. At age fifty, every man has the face he deserves. - *George Orwell*
7. I have everything I had twenty years ago, only it's all a little bit lower. - *Gypsy Rose Lee*
8. Middle age is when a narrow waist and a broad mind begin to change places. - *Author Unknown*
9. Middle age is when your age starts to show around your middle. - *Bob Hope*
10. Youth is a wonderful thing. What a crime to waste it on children. - *George Bernard Shaw*
11. Thirty-five is when you finally get your head together and your body starts falling apart. - *Caryn Leschen*
12. Some people, no matter how old they get, never lose their beauty - they merely move it from their faces into their hearts. - *Martin Buxbaum*

Discussion

1. Are you afraid of getting old? Why or why not?
2. How old do you want to live to be? Do you want to **live to the ripe old age of 100**? Why or why not?
3. Where do you hope to live when you get old? Do you expect to live with your children? Will you live on your own? What would you prefer?
4. What hobbies and interests will you pursue when you retire?
5. Do you have any living grandparents? How old are they? Are they in good health? Where do they live? How often do you see them? Do you worry about their health?
6. How do you feel about your parents growing older?
7. If your retired parents or parents-in-law wanted to move in with you, how would you feel? What would be the advantages and disadvantages? When you are retirement age, how would you feel about living with your children and their spouses?
8. If your parents could no longer care for themselves, would you let them live with you or put them in a nursing home?
9. Do you think it is fair for a family to have older parents live with them? Do you think this added cost takes money away from the children's future?
10. If one of your parents **passed away**, would it be okay for the surviving spouse to remarry? Why or why not? If your spouse did, would you be interested in remarrying?

11. Is there anything you would especially like to do for your parents after they retire?

12. What are some advantages and disadvantages of **nursing homes**? Will you make arrangements for your parents into go to a nursing home? Would you live in a nursing home? You are used to being self-sufficient. Could you be happy if you had to **be cared for**? Would **being cared for** constantly hurt your pride?

13. Many western countries, especially in Europe, have an aging population these days: there will soon be more old people than young people. Is this also true of your country? What problems will this cause? How will it affect your country? How will it affect your life in the future?

14. At what age do most people in your country retire? At what age would you like to retire?

15. If people are still able to (and want to) work, should they be required to retire when they reach a certain age? Should older workers be forced to retire from their jobs in order to make way for younger workers?

16. Do you know any people who continued to work part-time after they retired? What kind of work do they do? Will you continue to work part-time when you retire? If so, what kind of part-time work will you do?

17. How do people prepare for retirement? What are some of the things that you will consider before retiring? How are your parents preparing themselves for retirement? Do they talk about it? How are you preparing?

18. Is it a good idea for older people to consider having cosmetic surgery to look younger? Would you consider it for yourself or your spouse? Why or why not?

19. Do you think that there is any valuable information the older generation can give to young adults in these modern times? Are there many things that **senior citizens** and **the elderly** can teach the young, or are they hopelessly **out of touch** by the time they reach their senior years? Have you learned anything from older family members? How has the information been useful?

20. What are some medical problems that are common among **senior citizens**? How can they be prevented?

21. At what age do you consider a person to be old?

22. What are some things an older person can do to look and feel younger?

23. Who is the oldest person you know? Describe their physical and emotional condition.

24. Is there an **elderly** person you admire? What do you admire the most about them?

25. Do you know someone who **is really aging gracefully**? Do you know any older people who seem to be to **be full of life and vigor**? What do they do? What is their secret?

26. In general, are young adults more selfish than their parents and grandparents? As people age, do they generally become more aware of and caring for others?

27. In many countries, there is a tradition of choosing leaders who are quite old. Do you think that older people make better leaders? Explain.

28. In most countries women live an average of five to six years longer than men. For example, in the US, life expectancy is 81 for women, but only 75 for men. In your opinion, what explains the difference in life expectancy for women and men?

LESSON

9 What a Rip-off!

Language Points

to get ripped off / a rip-off / rip-off prices

I can't believe you paid $200 for those running shoes. I think you got ripped off.

a knock-off / a fake / imitation / counterfeit / copycat brands

In the market, they are selling all kinds of **knock-offs** of famous luxury and some of them are pretty convincing.

a con man / a con artist / a rip-off artist

The salesman is a real **con artist**. He guaranteed that I was buying this luxury watch at a great price, but now I know that it's a fake. .

to be reasonably/unreasonably priced / exorbitantly priced

This stereo was **reasonably priced**. I don't think I paid too much for it.

intellectual property / IP

Some musicians complain that downloading music from the Internet for free is illegal. They say that the music that they have created is their intellectual property, and listeners should have to pay to access it.

to pirate / piracy

Some musicians complain that some of their fans are guilty of piracy. They copy their music illegally.

to plagiarize / to plagiarize material

If you plagiarize someone else's ideas and pretend that they are your own, you could get into a lot of trouble. At university, you could fail the course or even get suspended.

to spare no expense (to do/achieve something)

She spares no expense to make herself look good. She buys expensive clothes and cosmetics, and goes to the beauty salon regularly.

to bootleg / a bootleg recording

The Beatles recently sued a record company for selling a bootlegged recording of a concert they gave in Hamburg, Germany in 1962.

Dialogue

A woman is talking with her co-worker from another department.

Melanie: Hey, Judy. How's it going?
Judy: Not bad. Did you have a nice weekend?
Melanie: Sure. The weather was just perfect, wasn't it? Hey, I like your new purse!
Judy: Do you? I just got it on Sunday. It wasn't cheap, but I really liked it, so...
Melanie: You mean it's a REAL Chanel?!
Judy: Of course. What did you think it was?

Melanie: Well, I just assumed it was fake. I didn't think people actually bought real luxury leather goods anymore. I mean, **the knock-offs** are so convincing. Why would you...

Judy: I know, but... I just disagree with **counterfeiting**. People work hard to build up their brand's image, and then some con artists come along and try to get a free ride. That's low, isn't it?

Melanie: Yeah, I guess so, but it's not as if anyone cares. I mean, everybody buys fake designer goods. Who wants to pay $2000 for a purse when you can get one that looks identical for $40? Do you really think the prices people charge for designer goods are reasonable?

Judy: It depends how you look at it. You're not paying for the materials. You're paying for the design and the **brand recognition**. When people see this handbag, they know it's a Chanel. And that brand has a certain image. It says 'style' and 'luxury'. People get that kind of impression.

Melanie: No, they don't. They probably think it's a fake, just like I did. So, why spend all that money? It just doesn't make any sense.

Judy: Anyways, I didn't buy it. My husband did. And I certainly don't want him to buy me a fake, do I?

Melanie: Ah, well, that's a whole different story.

Comprehension

1. With whom do you agree with more, Melanie or Judy? Why?
2. Do you think that you are the kind of person who **spares no expense** to own the best of everything, or are you satisfied with products that are more **reasonably priced**?
3. What is the most **unreasonably priced** product you've ever come across?
4. When you see someone with an expensive-looking purse, watch, or other product, do you assume it's genuine or fake? Why?
5. Why do you think brand name products are in such high demand? Is it because they are better quality than other products? Or are there other reasons that so many people want to own (or appear to own) luxury brand products?
6. Have you ever bought fake designer goods? What did you buy? Were you satisfied with the quality?
7. Do you think that producing fake designer goods is a serious crime? Why or why not? How about purchasing them?
8. If you were a fashion designer and you found out that people had been making large amounts of money copying your designs, how would you feel? What would you do?
9. Do you prefer wearing clothing with logos that are conspicuous? Why or why not?

Activity A

Spare No Expense

If you were in the market for the best quality products money could buy, what brands would you purchase? With your classmate(s), test your knowledge of brands and consider the questions that follow.

Product	Brand Name
Digital Camera	
In-line Skates	
Cellular Phone	
Home Theatre	
Purse	
Running Shoes	
Sports Clothing	
Cosmetics	
Dress Shoes	
Watch	
Laptop Computer	
Pen	
Sunglasses	
MP3 Players	

1. Choose three products for which you did not choose the same company as your classmate(s) and explain to them why the products you chose are better.
2. With your classmate(s) guess the approximate retail price of the items and discuss whether this price is reasonable and justifiable.
3. Which of the items you listed do you think you will ever realistically own? Which do you only dream of owning?
4. If these brands were not famous, would you still purchase these items? Why?

Activity B

Priorities

Think about what your priorities are when you buy various products. Choose items from the list on the left. Discuss with your classmate(s) which factors are most important to you and why.

Product	Priorities
1 Car	• Brand Name
2 Bag	• Brand Image
3 Formal Clothing	• Workmanship / Durability
4 Underwear	• Design / Style
5 Cellular Phone	• Colour
6 Dress Shoes	• Price
7 Sports Equipment	• Functionality
8 Stereo Equipment	• Ease of Use
9 Television	• Special Features
10 Computer	• Simplicity
11 Furniture	• Prominent Logo
12 Refrigerator	• Comfort
13 Hair Drier	• Other
14 Cosmetics	
15 Perfume / Cologne	
16 Shampoo	
17 Jewellery	

Discussion

1. Have you ever **plagiarized** material for an essay, project, or proposal? Is this practice common? Do you think it is wrong? Why or why not?

2. In most reputable Western universities, there are strict rules regarding **plagiarism**, and breaking them can result in expulsion from the university. What sorts of rules exist in universities in your country againt plagiarism? Are they strictly enforced? Is plagiarism a problem at universities in your country?

3. Do you buy a lot of **knock-offs**? What **knock-offs** have you bought recently? Are you satisfied with the quality?

4. When was the last time you felt you **got ripped off**? What did you buy? How much did it cost?

5. Have you ever been the victim of **con man**? What happened? How much money did you spend?

6. What things in your country are **unreasonably priced**? Do you often buy something even though you know that it is unreasonably priced?

7. If a student is proven to have **plagiarized** a project at university, what would be the suitable punishment? Should the student fail the assignment, fail the course, or be suspended for the semester?

8. How would you define '**intellectual property**'?

9. Do you think that intellectual property should be protected under the law?

10. What products are commonly pirated in your country?

11. Are there any **copycat brands** in your country (products or logos that are intentionally designed to look like more famous brands)? What do you think of them? Do you buy a lot of copycat brands?

12. Copying other people's work is also common in the music industry. Do you know of any songs that sound similar to other famous songs?

13. Is **bootlegging** music, software and movies common in your country? Where are bootlegs commonly sold?

14. Sometimes copyrighting intellectual property can become ridiculous, as when McDonald's tried to prevent other companies from using the prefixes 'Mc' or 'Mac' as part of a product name. What do you think? Do companies have a right to claim such common things as their own?

15. Do you believe that a writer owns the words and ideas he or she uses?

16. What file sharing programs do you use? What do you download: music, software, movies, picture files? Do you feel like you're doing something wrong? Why or why not?

17. If you liked music, movies or software that you'd downloaded, would you buy the CD, DVD or software?

18. Do you think that software is worth the **exorbitant** prices that some big software companies charge for their products?

19. Is **pirating** music, software, or movies a 'victimless crime'?

10 Can You Handle It?

Language Points

to stick to your guns / to stick to something (i.e., a decision, a commitment)

My parents tried to change my mind, but I stuck to my guns. I decided to drop out of school to be the leader singer in my rock band.

to cave in

I didn't cave in, even though my parents put pressure on me to change my major.

to stand on (one's) own two feet

I really feel that I need to stand on my own two feet and stop relying on others.

no one/man is an island

I believe that no one is an island. Nobody can thrive if he is alone and isolated from other people.

to strike out on one's own

I decided to strike out on my own. I no longer live with my parents because I wanted to become independent.

to live on one's own

I live on my own. I moved out from my parents house a few weeks ago.

mama's boy

I'm 30 years old now, and I'm fed up with all the jokes about being a mama's boy.

to rely on someone / to be reliant / self-reliant / over-reliant

I'm ready to stop relying so heavily on others to take care of me. I want to be self-reliant. I want to be able to do things and make decisions by myself.

Dialogue

A young man talks with his mother over the phone.

Jason: ...Mom, I just don't know if Medicine is for me.

Claire: Jason, your father and I are very disappointed by all of this. Why would you want to change your major? I mean, you're in one of the best medical schools in the country. You're doing well. It just doesn't make any sense to us, Jason. What's wrong? Is it a girl?

Jason: No, Mom. It's not a girl. I just don't want to be a doctor. I've thought about it, and I know I won't be enjoying it, you know, ten or twenty years down the road. True, I might be working in a big hospital, and helping a lot of people. But I don't think I'll be happy.

Claire: But why, Jason? We've spent so much money to get you where you are, and now you want to throw it all away? You must understand why we're having such a hard time accepting this. Your father and I just want you to make something of yourself. We don't want you to be facing retirement in forty years and feeling like you haven't accomplished anything with your life. If you've had a successful career as a doctor, you will really have done something significant, Jason.

Jason: I know. I'm sorry, but my heart's just not in it. I never really wanted to be a doctor. I'm just sorry that I never realized it before.

Claire: I don't know what we're going to do with you. Well, what DO you want to be, Jason? What in heaven's name are you going to do now?

Jason: Don't get upset, Mom. I've got a plan. I'm going to switch my major to Computer Science. That's always been my passion.

Claire: Computer Science?! Oh, for goodness sake, Jason. What are you going on about?

Jason: Listen, Mom. I've got it all worked out. In three years, I'll have graduated, and that's exactly when Nevada Games will be hiring people. My friend who works there said that they're developing a new game console, and after the launch, they're going to be needing people to develop new games for it.

Claire: Video games? Oh, Jason, really. You're dropping out of medical school to make video games? You've had some silly ideas before, Jason, but this really takes the cake.

Jason: When I'm making six figures and having a lot of fun doing it, you'll understand. Come on, Mom, you know how much I love video games.

Claire: Jason, I've heard quite enough! I want you to think very carefully about what you're doing. Your father and I will talk about this, and he'll be phoning you tonight at about 9, so you'd better think of something sensible to say to him. Goodbye, Jason.

Jason: Okay, I'll talk to you later. Don't expect that I will have changed my mind. Mom... Hello? Mom?

Comprehension

1. Could this kind of dialogue between a mother and her son take place in your country? If the conversation took place between you and your mother/father, what do you think the outcome would be?

2. Do you think that Jason's mother is justified in her arguments? Which of her points to you agree or disagree with?

3. To what extent do you think Jason's parents have a right to decide their son's future?

4. At what point do you think grown-up children are ready to make their own decisions? At what age will / did you start to make your own decisions?

5. Who decided what your major at university would be, you or your parents? Did you have any disagreements about which degree you should take?

6. Even if our parents are older and wiser, does this mean that they always know what is best for us? Is it important for us to make our own decisions even if they do turn out to be wrong?

7. Do you trust your parents' decisions when it comes to your love life? Describe the differences, if any, between the people your parents want(ed) you to date, and the sorts of people you want(ed) to?

8. Did you ever have a big difference of opinion with your parents over your future plans? What happened? Did you **stick to your guns** or **cave in**?

9. Do you think that parents always try to treat their sons and daughters like children no matter how old they are? Do your parents still treat you this way? Give examples.

10. If parents continually try to push their children to be what they want them to be, is it likely that the children will simply end up rebelling against their parents and resenting them?

11. Should parents try to encourage their children to become independent as soon as possible? Why do you think so?

12. Do you think that parents have an obligation to protect their children (even their adult children) from making mistakes, or should parents allow their children to learn things on their own by making mistakes?

Activity A

Survival Quiz

If you were thrown out in the middle of nowhere with nothing but a few supplies, could you survive? With your classmate(s), discuss the following questions and try to figure out the best answers. Try to justify your answer with a reasonable explanation. Then check your answers to see if you'd survive in the wild.

Answer

1 The best way to locate water in the wild is to:

A. Dig at least three feet into the sand
B. Look for wind patterns when tree branches blow
C. Follow some bees or flies

2 When you're melting snow to get water you should never:

A. Melt the snow on a fire or camp stove
B. Use snow that comes from below the surface
C. Melt the snow on a rock

Answer

3 It's easier to start a fire with wet wood than dry wood.

A. True
B. False

4 Which of the following is most vital to your survival:

A. Shelter
B. Fire
C. Food

5 The more you try to clean a wound in the wild, the more likely you are to cause infection.

A. True
B. False

6 The first step in testing whether a plant is edible is to:

A. Chew a small amount for five minutes without swallowing.
B. Rub a small amount of the plant on a sensitive part of your body.
C. Swallow a small piece of the plant and wait eight hours.

7 Desert areas are best defined as having:

A. Hot weather all the time.
B. Hot weather in the summer and cold weather in the winter.
C. Hot weather during the day and cold weather at night.

8 The part of your body that loses heat fastest is:

A. Your feet
B. Your nose
C. Your head

9 You should never wear cotton as an insulator.

A. True
B. False

10 The best way to deal with a snake bite is to:

A. Suck the venom out with your mouth
B. Cut out the venom by cutting an "X" across the fang punctures
C. First, do no damage to the wound

Answers

① **C -** Locate / follow bees or flies. Bees and flies instinctively return to wet areas.

② **A -** Don't melt the snow on a fire or camp stove. Why waste valuable fuel when there are easier ways to melt snow?

③ **B -** False. Wet or green wood is very difficult to light. Dry ground fall will light with the least amount of effort.

④ **A -** Shelter. If you get cold and wet, or over-heated in the hot sun, your body will get tired and you will be unable to do other things to keep yourself alive.

⑤ **A -** True. In the wilderness, you are unlikely to have the proper resources to clean a wound well. The best thing to do is stop the bleeding, keep the wound covered, changing the dressing periodically, and let your body take care of fighting any infection.

⑥ **B -** Rub a small amount of the plant on a sensitive part of your body. If a plant is toxic, the poisons will likely cause a rash or itchiness on sensitive skin.

⑦ **C -** Hot weather during the day and cold weather at night. If you do not take proper precautions in the desert at night, you may find yourself dealing with a case of hypothermia.

⑧ **C -** Your head. Put a hat on, and you'll retain a lot of your body heat.

⑨ **A -** True. Cotton does not conduct moisture well, and instead holds it close to your skin, cooling it, and causing you to lose heat.

⑩ **C -** At first, don't damage the wound. Snake poison does the most damage when it is circulating around your body. Doing anything to the site of the bite will stimulate circulation and move the poison around your body quicker. Remain calm and make your way slowly to medical aid.

Results

7 to 10 → **You're tough and ready for almost anything.**

3 to 6 → **You might survive. Then again, you might not.**

0 to 2 → **You'd better stick to the city.**

Activity B

Standing on Your Own Two Feet

Ideally, people gain independence from their parents in progressive stages. Although there may be slight differences between people, everyone undergoes these steps in more or less the same order and at more or less the same age. In fact, if we happen to see individuals who deviate too much from this understood 'schedule', we may feel that there is something wrong with either them or their parents.

On the time line below, place the number of each developmental milestone from the list. Then discuss the questions that follow with your classmates.

Birth · ½ · 1 · 1½ · 2 · 2½ · 3 · 4 · 5 · 6 · 7 · 8 · 9 · 10 · 11 · 12 · 13 · 14 · 15 · 16 · 17 · 18 · 19 · 20 · 21

1 Live alone	2 Stop using a baby bottle
3 Use public transportation on their own	4 Drive
5 Be responsible their own finances	6 Drink alcohol
7 Take responsibility for their own grades	8 Sleep alone
9 Stay home alone	10 Walk somewhere alone
11 Walk without holding an adult's hand	12 Go on dates
13 Feed themselves	14 Go to the toilet unassisted
15 Make important life decisions	16 Work

1. Have you ever met overprotective parents? How did they treat their children? What effect did this have on the children?

2. Did your parents let you do things when you felt you were ready to take them on? Or did they rush you into responsibilities?

3. Many young people want to live alone before they get married. Why do you think parents are so reluctant to allow this? What sorts of skills must a person possess in order to live alone successfully?

4. At what age do Western parents give various kinds of independence to their children? How does this compare with the situation in your home country?

5. Many Westerners make a nursery room for their newborns and have them sleep alone even a few weeks after birth. What do you think of this? What effects might it have on children as they grow up?

6. There are laws dictating at what age people can drive, have sex, smoke, and drink alcohol. Do you think the age limits that have been set up are reasonable? Are these laws tough enough and enforced sufficiently?

7. Choose three items from the list above and explain what skills or character traits are necessary prerequisites for each one.

Activity C

No One Is an Island

With the exception of a few hermits, castaways, and people who have chosen to live 'off the grid', none of us is entirely independent. With your classmate(s), discuss the following questions about the people who help you live your life.

1 Where do you go to get your hair cut? Why do you go to that salon? Have you ever had your hair permed, dyed, or straightened? If so, how much did it cost and how long did it take? Were you satisfied with the results? Why or why not?

2 Where do you (or your parents) get your (their) car serviced? Do you know anything about cars and car engines? Would you like to learn?

3 Do you feel nervous when you have to have dental work done? Have you ever had braces put on your teeth? Have you ever had a really painful experience in a dentist's chair?

4 When was the last time you had a medical check-up? Do you think you are usually in good health? What are some of your biggest health concerns?

5 Do you do your own laundry or does someone do it for you? Do you use a laundry service? If so, where do you get your clothes laundered?

6 Where do you get your clothes dry-cleaned? Do you get a good deal or do you have to pay too much? What makes you say so?

7 If you could afford it, would you like to have your house cleaned or your meals cooked for you? What do you think would be a reasonable fee for such services?

8 Do you enjoy having your picture taken? Are you camera shy? Why or why not? When was the last time you had your picture taken by a professional photographer? Were you satisfied with the results? Why or why not?

9 Have you ever had a manicure or pedicure? Is this kind of service only for women or is it alright for men to have it done as well? What makes you say so?

10 Have you ever had a professional massage? Where is a good place to get a massage?

11 Have you ever had to get your computer fixed? If so, what was the problem? Where is the best place to go to have work done on your computer?

Discussion

1. What does being independent mean to you? At what age did (or will) you **strike out on your own**? At what age did (will) you become fully independent?
2. What are (or will be) be the best things about being independent? What are the downsides?
3. Some people go directly from living at home to getting married without any time **living on their own**. Do such people ever experience true independence? Would you want to live on your own? Why or why not?
4. What are the pros and cons of living with your parents until you're married? How about **living on your own**?
5. Why do you think that most people crave independence even when it means that life might be more challenging?

6. When a person becomes independent, they are faced with a whole range of new responsibilities. Which do you think is the most challenging of these responsibilities?

7. According to the law, people become responsible for their own actions at the age of 18. As different people mature at different rates, do you think that there should be some flexibility regarding this age?

8. Many people say that girls mature faster than boys emotionally. Do you think this is true? Why or why not?

9 Who do you think is usually more independent: men or women? Do you think that a lot of men are **mama's boys**?

10. Some people never seem to mature enough to be independent. What qualities or skills must a person acquire to enable them to be independent?

11. When you were younger, did you envy any of your friends who had greater freedom than you? What was it about their lives that you envied?

12. It is said that '**no man is an island**' (John Donne - 1624). What do you think this quote means? As human beings, is it natural to be at least partly dependent on others?

13. Do you consider yourself to be an independent thinker? To what extent do you think other people influence your views and opinions?

14. What is one responsibility that you would like to get rid of? What is one responsibility that you would like to have?

15. How do you think attitudes toward independence in Western countries are different from attitudes in your home country? In your opinion, what are the main differences?

16. Do you think that young people, and young women in particular, are discouraged from being independent?

17. Is personal independence overrated?

18. Is there anyone you know who is truly independent? What gave you this impression of them?

19. Why is it that people generally don't like eating or going to movies by themselves? Have you ever done this? Did you mind the experience?

20. How much time, on average, do you spend alone per week? Are you happy with this or do you need more / less time alone?

21. Are you a **self-reliant** person? Or do you rely on someone or some people? Who? And for what?

22. Do you feel that you are **over-reliant** on anyone?

LESSON

11 Getting Away

Language Points

overwhelming

He tried to climb one of the tallest mountains in the Canadian Rockies, but the task was too overwhelming and he had to give up.

breathtaking

Our hotel room in the Swiss Alps had breathtaking views of the mountains and lakes from every room.

go trekking

He went trekking in the Amazon jungle, the Gobi desert, and the mountains of Nepal. He really enjoys the challenge of journeying on foot, especially on difficult terrain.

expedition

Yesterday I lay on the beach all afternoon, but today I'm either going to go on a shopping expedition or a fishing expedition.

off the beaten track

Do you prefer famous resorts and tourist locations or places that are off the beaten track – places where there are no crowds of people?

a hellish (experience, trip, time, etc.) / a nightmare

I had a hellish trip. I lost my passport. Then I missed my airplane and had to sleep in the airport. I wish I'd stayed home.

a travel companion

My best friend from university was also my travel companion when I hitchhiked through Europe.

to travel light

I like to travel light when I go abroad. I only need a pair of pants, a couple shirts, a pair of shoes and my underwear.

to take / bring everything but the kitchen sink

We're only going to the resort for the weekend. Why do you have three bags? You're bringing everything but the kitchen sink.

Reading

Places to Visit Before You Die

In 2002, the BBC "Holiday" program polled 20,000 viewers to find out opinions on what places everyone should visit before they die. The results for four categories are as follows:

The Best Natural Wonder: The Grand Canyon

Famous for its **overwhelming** size, intricate and colorful landscape, and **breathtaking**, majestic vistas, the Grand Canyon is a steep-sided gorge stretching 450 kilometers along the Colorado River in the U.S. state of Arizona. Known to native Americans, the region's original inhabitants, as the "mountain lying down," the canyon reaches a depth of 1.6 km at some points. Sightseeing from the canyon rim, whitewater rafting, and hiking – every year, hundreds of hikers make the trip down to the river on foot – are especially popular with tourists. Despite its beauty, visiting the Grand Canyon can be dangerous. Many hikers, overestimating their fitness level, become dehydrated and confused and have to be rescued. Furthermore, over 600 deaths have occurred in the canyon since the 1870s, usually the result of overly zealous photographers falling to their deaths, airplane collisions within the canyon, or drowning in the Colorado River.

The Best City: Cape Town and Table Mountain

Each year close to two million tourists visit Cape Town, drawn to its good climate, beautiful natural setting and beaches. Table Mountain, which can be reached by hiking or cable car, provides a spectacular view of the city and the ocean. Below the mountains are beautiful sandy beaches, known for gorgeous sunsets and big-wave surfing. Whale and dolphin watching are also popular tourist attractions. The city is also noted for its architectural heritage, which combines the architectural traditions of the Netherlands, Germany and France.

The Best Sunshine Destination: Florida and Disneyworld

Walt Disney died in December 1966 after spending an evening with his brother working on a new Florida theme park. In the more than 40 years since his death, the theme park Disney never lived to see has grown into the most visited (tens of millions of people visit it each year) and largest recreational resort in the world. Disney World now includes the Animal Kingdom, a wildlife and animal conservation theme park featuring safaris, rafting and **trekking**, as well as two water parks with water coasters, wave pools, speed slides, raft rides, tube slides, snorkeling among tropical fish and reefs, and sandy beaches. The park is located in Florida, known as the "Sunshine State" for its warm, sunny weather and sandy beaches.

The Best Man-Made Wonder: The Taj Mahal

Most famous for its spectacular white domed marble and tile mausoleum, the Taj Mahal, or "Crown Palace," based on the Banks of the Yamura River in Agra, India, is visited each year by over 4 million tourists, including more than 200,000 from overseas. Completed in 1648, following 22 years of construction under Mughal Emperor Shah Jahan, the structure combines elements from Persian, Turkish, Indian and Islamic architectural styles. In 1983, UNESCO declared it as a World Heritage Site and "one of the universally admired masterpieces" in the world. Legend has it that Shah Jahan had planned to construct a second Taj Mahal in black marble on the other side of the river, but conflict with his sons interrupted his plans.

Natural Wonders

1. The Grand Canyon, USA
2. Great Barrier Reef, Queensland, Australia
3. South Island, New Zealand
4. Canadian Rockies
5. Uluru (Ayers Rock), Australia

Cities

1. Cape Town and Table Mountain
2. Las Vegas
3. Sydney, Australia
4. New York
5. Venice

Sunshine Destinations

1. Florida and Disneyland
2. Hawaii
3. Barbados
4. Bali
5. French Polynesia (Bora Bora)

Man-Made Wonders

1. Taj Mahal, Agra, India
2. Golden Temple at Amritsar, Punjab, India
3. Chichen Itza, Yucatan Peninsula, Mexico
4. Machu Picchu, Peru
5. Petra, Jordan

Comprehension

1. What do know about the places on the four lists? Are there any places that you have not heard of or know very little about?

2. From the 20 places listed, choose the five that you would most like to visit. Explain your choices, starting with the one you would like to visit the most.

3. Do you agree with the viewers' choices for each category? In your opinion, are there some other locations that are overrated and do not deserve to be on the list? Are there some places that you think should have made the lists?

4. What kinds of negative and positive consequences does a high amount of tourism have on an area?

5. Do you (or would you) make an effort to learn about the culture, history, and geography of an area before you visit it?

6. List the most popular foreign tourist destinations for the people of your country. What is it about each of these places that is attractive?

7. Why do you think people usually seem to want to see the most popular tourist attractions in a country (which are 'made for tourists') rather than the authentic local sites that might not be so well known?

8. Do you consider sampling the local food and drink to be an important part of experiencing the culture of a country? Why or why not?

9. Do you (or would you) bring food with you when you travel?

10. Who is the most memorable local person you've met while travelling?

Activity A

Dream Vacation

With your classmate(s), discuss which of the following options you would choose for your dream vacation. Give reasons for your choices.

1. Length of Trip

☐ A year or more ☐ 6 -12 months ☐ 1 - 6 months ☐ 1 month or less

2. Budget

☐ Luxury ☐ First class ☐ Comfortable ☐ Low Budget

3. Travel Style

☐ Resort ☐ Backpacking ☐ Eco-tour ☐ Condo Rental
☐ Home-/Farm-stay ☐ Package tour ☐ Cruise
☐ Self-planned Tour ☐ Expedition ☐ Other

4. Location(s)

☐ North America	☐ Western Europe	☐ Northern Africa	☐ Southeast Asia
☐ Central America	☐ Northern Europe	☐ Africa	☐ Arctic
☐ South America	☐ Eastern Europe	☐ Central Asia	☐ Mediterranean
☐ South Pacific	☐ Middle East	☐ Eastern Asia	☐ Australia / N.Z.

5. Activities

☐ Museums	☐ Camping / Hiking	☐ Wildlife Viewing	☐ Breweries Tour
☐ Mountaineering	☐ Historical Sites	☐ Fishing	☐ Photography
☐ Gastronomical Tour	☐ Rock/ice climbing	☐ Golf	☐ Safari
☐ Wineries Tour	☐ Gambling	☐ Sailing/Boating	☐ Diving
☐ Expeditions	☐ Distilleries Tour	☐ skiing/snowboarding	☐ Other

6. Attractions

☐ Famous attractions ☐ Popular attractions ☐ Off the beaten track ☐ No attractions

7. Food

☐ food from your home country ☐ Western food ☐ Local food

8. Travelling Companion(s)

☐ Alone ☐ Spouse ☐ Family ☐ Friend(s) ☐ Lover

After you have discussed your travel plans with your classmate(s), give a brief presentation to the class.

Activity B

Foreigners on the Loose

Divide into two brainstorming groups. Organize your ideas with your group and be prepared to report your results to the class.

Group A: "Home Away From Home" Team

Think of as many events, experiences, situations and incidents as possible that would make for a positive experience for a foreigner in your country. If a foreigner wanted to have a fantastic vacation here, what should they do, see, eat, wear, and visit? How could someone easily adapt to the lifestyle of your country if they were planning to live here? List as many things as possible.

Group B: "Hell on Earth" Team

Think of as many events, experiences, situations and incidents as possible that would make for a negative experience for a foreigner in your country. Under what circumstances would a person have a terrible vacation? What might be hard for a foreigner to deal with? What kind of culture shock might someone have? List as many things as possible..

Activity C

Work in pairs or small groups. Players take turns, moving from the start to the finish. Flip two coins. (Two heads = 3 spaces. One head and one tail = 2 spaces. Two tails = 1 space.) When a player lands on a square, he/she must talk for 30 seconds on the topic in the box.

Start

1 the qualities of a perfect travel companion	**2** the last time you traveled abroad	**3** the best or worst airline	**4** the best things to buy at the duty free shop
5 a great place for a romantic holiday	**6** a great place for a skiing vacation.	**7** a modern, exciting city you'd like to visit	**8** a European country you'd like to visit
9 a great tropical island you'd like to visit	**10** some things that you should always bring with you when you travel	**11** the things you miss about your home country when traveling	**12** a great place to enjoy spectacular natural scenery
13 your opinion on travel packages	**14** your opinion about traveling alone	**15** relaxing vs. active vacations	**16** the best souvenir you've ever bought or received

17
your opinion about going on a cruise

18
your favorite holiday destination in your home country

19
the best holiday you've ever taken in your home country

20
the best holiday destination in your home country for foreigners

21
winter vs. summer vacations

22
the pros and cons of taking a year off from university (or work) to travel

23
why foreigners should visit your country

24
a place you've always wanted to visit.

25
your most frustrating travel experience

26
the most beautiful place you've ever seen

27
your favorite city in the world

28
your favorite city in your country

Finish

Discussion

Past Experiences: Traveling and Living Abroad

1. Have you ever been abroad? What foreign country / countries have you visited? Was it for vacation or study? Where did you go? How long did you stay there? Would you like to go back to the same place? Do you wish you were still there, or are you happy to have returned?
2. What is the most interesting place you have ever visited?
3. What's the most beautiful place you've ever been to?
4. Describe your best trip and worst trip.
5. Have you ever had a **hellish travel experience** (i.e., lost luggage, stolen money or passports, delayed or missed flights, sickness or injury)? Discuss your worst **travel nightmare**. Was the problem resolved in the end?

6. Which of the places you've been would you recommend to your friends? Have you been anywhere that you think everyone should see before they die?

7. Which of the places you've been would you discourage your friends from visiting? Why?

Future: Travel Plans and Travel Preferences

1. Are you planning on going anywhere in the near future, either for vacation or for study? If so, where are you going? Who are you going with? How long do you plan to stay? What do you plan to do there?

2. What countries / places would you most like to visit? Why do you want to go there? Do you think you will ever go there?

3. If you had $100,000, where would you go on holiday, how long would you stay, and what would you do? If you had $10,000? $2,000?

4. Would you ever consider taking time off to travel around the world? If so, how long?

5. If you could go any place in the world for the weekend, where would it be?

6. Where would you expect to encounter:

- the warmest hospitality
- the rudest service
- the most vibrant lifestyle
- the most relaxed lifestyle
- the most delicious food
- the most handsome men / the most beautiful women
- the most fashionable people
- the best shopping
- the best beaches
- the best nightlife
- the best nature
- the most spectacular scenery
- the most exciting outdoor activities

LESSON

12 Incommunicado

Language Points

to be contactable
You can call me anytime of day or night. I'm always contactable.

cell phone etiquette
I can't believe he let his cell phone ring in the movie theatre. And then he answered it! He clearly doesn't understand cell phone etiquette.

face-to-face communication
I enjoy speaking on the phone and sending people email, but face-to-face communication is much more meaningful.

fabricate personal details
Many people fabricate personal details when they enter information on the internet. They lie about their age, appearance, and background.

to give someone the silent treatment / to give someone the cold shoulder
When my girlfriend gets angry with me, she gives me the silent treatment. It's like torture.

to get in touch / to get in contact / to keep in touch with someone
My friend left a couple of months ago to study in the US. I've been keeping in touch with him by instant messenger.

to get one's point across / to make one's point
when you write an essay, you must get your point across. If you don't, your professor will give you a poor grade.

Reading

Internet Addiction

The Internet has brought about **profound** changes in the way we communicate, do business and find information. If we step back and consider all of the things that we can use the Internet to do, it is truly **staggering**. However, as with so many things, if people over-use or **misuse** it, the Internet can become a destructive force in their lives.

For some people, the computer world seems more attractive than their real world. They choose to spend large amounts of time interacting with people on-line, rather than with their real-life friends, spouse and children. Spending several hours a day on-line in chat rooms, viewing pornography, gambling, playing on-line games, e-trading, or just surfing, they insulate themselves from their responsibilities and relationships in the real world. Internet addiction causes serious psychological problems, work and school problems, physical health problems, social isolation, and marital **discord**.

Although psychologists admit that Internet Addiction Disorder (or 'IAD' as it has become known) is not based on a physical dependence, like addiction to cigarettes, alcohol, or **illicit** drugs, they view IAD as an out-of-control behavior like **obsessive** eating, sex, work or exercise.

This obsession may threaten to **overwhelm** the Net addict's normal life. Even though the addict may be aware (at some level at least) that serious physical, social or psychological problems are being caused or **worsened** by their use of the Internet, they will continue to stay on-line. These problems, such as sleep **deprivation**, **marital** difficulties, **chronic** lateness for appointments, **neglect** of job or home responsibilities, and feelings of **abandonment** in significant others, will only continue to worsen until the Net addict is able to deal honestly with their problem.

Comprehension

1. What kind of role does the Internet play in your life? Do you find yourself using the Internet more and more these days?
2. According to the article, what are some of the problems that the Internet causes?
3. How many hours per day do you usually spend online? How many times per day do you check your e-mail? Do you think that you spend too much time online?
4. How is Internet addiction different from alcoholism or drug dependence?
5. Did reading this article change your opinion about the seriousness of Internet addiction? If so, in what ways?
6. Do you think IAD is becoming a serious problem in your country? Is it the government's responsibility to try and do more to combat the problem?
7. Do you know anyone who is an Internet addict? How about you? Do you ever find yourself neglecting sleep just to spend a couple more hours online?
8. The average child is now spending increasing amounts of time surfing the web and playing computer games. Is this likely to result in social problems as they get older? Say why you think so.
9. How could you recognize the fact that you were in danger of becoming a Net addict? Having recognized the fact, how could you treat the problem?
10. Do you think that the influence of the Internet on our lives is largely positive or negative? Say why you think so.

Activity A

Effective Communication

Are you an effective communicator? How well do you get your point across? Discuss which of the following you think are important for being an effective communicator? Say how each can contribute positively and negatively to effective communication.

Body language
Ratio of speaking to listening
Choice of words
Length of communication
Facial expression
Dress and grooming
Tone of voice
Amount of eye contact
Distance from each other
Other

Activity B

Cell Phone Addiction

Work with your classmate(s) and give yourselves the following simple test to find out whether you are addicted or in danger of becoming addicted to using your cell phone.

	Yes	No
1 When you get bored, you spend time playing games or selecting new ring tones.		
2 You enjoy customizing your phone with various accessories.		
3 You get annoyed when someone has the same ring tone as you.		
4 You look for any excuse to take pictures using your phone.		
5 You check your phone at least once every 30 minutes just in case you missed an important message.		
6 You feel very uncomfortable if you have to turn your phone off for any reason.		
7 You can send a text message quicker than you can make a phone call.		
8 You feel the need to update your cell phone as soon as a better one comes out (e.g. touch screen, 3G phone).		
9 You spend time comparing your phone with those of your friends.		
10 You like to let your phone ring for a while before you answer it so that you (and others) can enjoy the new tune that you selected.		
11 You feel envious when you see someone with a better cell phone than yours.		
12 You strongly feel that choosing the right cell phone is important because it says something about who you are.		

Scoring: For each question you answered 'yes' to, give yourself a point. If you end up with more than six points, you're in danger of being a cell phone addict.

Question

1. Do you remember what life was like before cell phones were invented?

2. Is it now hard to believe that people used to be able to communicate effectively without cell phones?

3. On average, how long do you spend each day using your cell phone (including text messaging, playing games, taking photos and using it as a mirror to check your appearance)?

4. When you choose a cell phone, what are the main criteria (e.g. size, color, easy of use, functions, etc.)?

5. Do you know anyone who doesn't have a cell phone? Do they have a good reason for not having one?

6. If you found out that a person (under 50 years old) didn't have a cell phone, would you think they were strange? Why or why not?

7. Nowadays, do you think that everyone is expected to be **contactable** 24 hours a day? Do you think that this is an infringement of our privacy?

8. The most recent innovation in cell phone technology is the video phone. Can you imagine what the next big innovation will be?

9. When do you prefer to send a text message and when do you prefer to make a phone call?

10. Do you ever get irritated by other people using their cell phones in public? What type of things irritate you?

11. Is public cell phone etiquette necessary? In what ways should people be considerate when using their cellphones in public?

12. Are you considerate towards other people when you use your cell phone in public? If not, why not?

Activity C

How Should I Put This?

Below is a list of communication situations. In each case discuss the pros and cons of each form of communication.

1. **Dumping your boyfriend or girlfriend**
   a) Face-to-face b) Text message c) Hand-written letter
2. **Birthday greetings**
   a) Phone call b) Hand-written card c) E-card
3. **Canceling an appointment with a friend**
   a) Text message b) Phone call c) E-mail
4. **Complaining about rude service in a shop**
   a) Shout at the assistant b) Shout at the manager c) Contact Head Office
5. **A stranger insults you in front of your friends for no reason**
   a) Swearing b) "Sign language" c) "Physical Communication"
6. **Sending a sexy message to your sweetheart**
   a) Scented letter b) Voice message c) Text message
7. **Getting advice from your friend**
   a) Messenger service b) Face-to-face c) E-mail
8. **Advertising your company's products**
   a) TV advertising b) Leaflets c) Internet pop-up ad
9. **Apologizing to your friend for missing their wedding**
   a) Hand-written apology b) Phone call c) Text message
10. **Making up with your boyfriend or girlfriend after cheating on him or her**
    a) Send flowers b) Face-to-face groveling c) Hand-written letter

Discussion

1. As we acquire an ever-increasing number of ways to communicate with each other, do these tend to supplement or replace **face-to-face communication**?

2. Aside from direct conversation, which is your favorite way to communicate these days (e.g. e-mail, text messaging, messenger service, etc.)?

3. Do you think that there is a tendency nowadays for people to use various types of indirect communication to avoid dealing with sensitive issues face-to-face?

4. Relative to other advanced countries, where does your country rank in terms of Internet use and technology? Is it ahead or behind most countries? What do you think explains the level of Internet use in your country?

5. Are you a naturally talkative person? Are you good at keeping in touch with your friends and relatives?

6. Do you still send hand-written letters? Do you think that there are some situations where a hand-written letter is preferable to other forms of communication? If so, explain why you think so?

7. Have you ever used Internet chat rooms? If so, did this ever lead to any face-to-face meetings?

8. When people meet in Internet chat rooms, it is common to **fabricate personal details**. Why do you think that people often lie about themselves on-line?

9. Do you ever feel awkward trying to communicate with people of different generations (such as your grandparents)? If so, why do you think this is?

10. It is said that over 90% of communication is non-verbal. Excluding written and verbal communication, can you think of some other major ways in which information is communicated?

11. How important do you think that body language is in daily communication? Are you good at reading other people's body language?

12. Did you ever get to know someone over the phone or through e-mail who turned out to be very different from what you'd expected when you finally met face-to-face?

13. Do you think that the ever-increasing number of devices available for keeping in touch with each other is helping us to become better communicators? Why or why not?

14. Do you think that some company employees tend to overuse Messenger or similar services? Do you think that some companies are justified in banning the use of this kind of software?

15. When video phones start to widely replace conventional phones, what do you think will be some of the pros and cons?

16. If you had to give up using one form of communication, which one would it be?

17. What are the characteristics of a good communicator?

18. Do people in different countries communicate differently? Are some communication technologies used more/less in your country than in others?

19. When you **get in touch with** friends who are living abroad, how do you do it? How often do you **contact** them?

20. If you have traveled or studied abroad, how did you **keep in touch** with your relatives? How often did you **contact** them?

21. Have you ever **given someone the silent treatment** for something they did? Has anyone ever given you the silent treatment? What had you done?

22. Do you consider yourself **contactable** 24 hours a day? If someone sent you a text message at 3:30 in the morning, would you answer it?

23. What are some unwritten rules of **cell phone etiquette**? Do you feel that most people follow these rules, or do most people break them?

LESSON

13 Creatures of Habit

Language Points

a creature of habit

I am a creature of habit. That's why I follow a fairly similar routine every day.

to do something automatically

I don't specifically remember locking the door this morning. I do it automatically without thinking. It's a habit.

to break a habit / to break out of a habit / to overcome a habit

I want to break out of the bad habits I've picked up in recent years.

to make a conscious effort (to do something / to change something / to break a habit)

Breaking habits takes a conscious effort. If you don't make a conscious effort, you will never break the habits.

to be / become set in one's ways

Some people are stubborn and set in their ways. They never want to change.

engrained

We need to make a conscious effort to change deeply engrained bad habits.

to be / stuck on something/ to be hooked on something

I'm hooked on alcohol. I go drinking every night.

to have an addictive personality

My friend has an addictive personality. She always seems to be getting addicted to one thing or another.

to be obsessed with someone

She is totally obsessed with him. She has all of his CDs, has his pictures on the wall, and writes him fan mail all the time.

Reading A

Creatures of Habit

We are all **creatures of habit**. Many of the activities that are part of our everyday routine, like tying our shoes, dialling familiar phone numbers, and brushing our teeth, are **done automatically**, without the intervention of our will, and most of the time without even entering into our conscious awareness. In fact, if you carefully examine your daily behaviour, it is tempting to see the majority of what we do everyday in terms of **habits we have picked up**. From the time we get up in the morning to our personal hygiene routine before bed, the bulk of our activity is a result of the habits that we have developed throughout our lives.

The habits that we form over the years each result from conscious choices. At some point in our lives, we made a conscious effort to learn a new behaviour, to try something new, or to mimic the behaviour of those around us. But with repetition, these behaviours became habits.

This ability to learn behaviours so thoroughly that they can become routine and do not require our conscious attention probably developed as a mechanism to free our attention for other, more important tasks, such as locating food and keeping alert to potential threats. Certainly, it goes without saying that if we had to focus our attention on the details of our lives, our nervous systems would be unable to cope with much else.

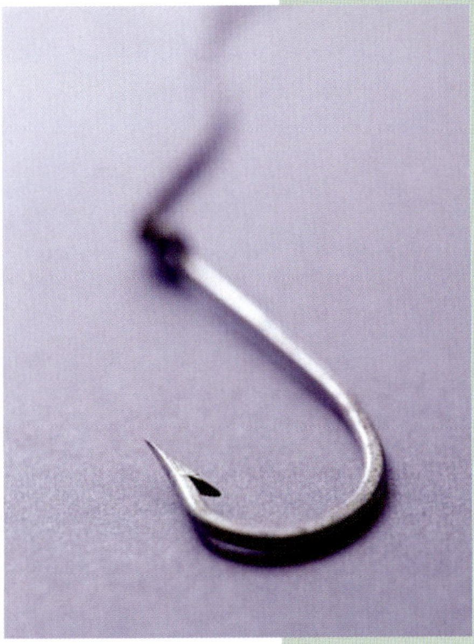

At some point, however, we may want to **make a conscious effort to break out of old habits** or adopt new ones when we have a shift in our priorities. It is at such times that we may encounter varying degrees of resistance. Habits become convenient, familiar, and comfortable. They become interwoven in complex ways with our behaviours, our emotions, and even with our ideas about who we are. We **become set in our ways** as time goes by, and habits become **engrained** and increasingly difficult to overcome. In our efforts to change our behaviour, we may go through a number of discouraging false starts, repeatedly falling back into our old patterns.

Overcoming the force of habit, especially those habits that we have had for extended periods of time, is a process that takes time. The important thing is to clearly articulate one's commitment to change a habit, clearly imagine the rewards associated with doing so, set reasonable, attainable goals, exercise our willpower, and be ready to experience a certain amount of discomfort and to encounter temptation. Don't succumb to the easy way out. If you allow yourself one slip, it is that much easier to slip again. With perseverance, however, it is possible to overcome even the most deeply engrained habits, and develop the new behaviours that will best serve us.

Comprehension

1. Are high school and university students under peer pressure to drink alcohol and smoke cigarettes?
2. What should parents tell their children about drinking alcohol and smoking cigarettes?
3. Do you consider tobacco more or less harmful to people than alcohol?
4. The researchers claim that there is no scientific basis for excluding alcohol and tobacco from the list of harmful drugs. Do you agree? Why or why not?
5. Would life in your country be different without alcohol and tobacco? How would your life be different if alcohol and tobacco were made illegal?
6. Do you believe that alcohol is harmful to society? Would society function better(or worse) without alcohol and tobacco?
7. Alcohol is a long-standing part of the culture in many countries. Is it acceptable for that reason?
8. Should the government play an active role in discouraging the use of alcohol and tobacco? Should they be made illegal? Should they be taxed more heavily?

Reading B

Alcohol, Tobacco, and Drugs

Research carried out in the UK ranks alcohol and tobacco among the ten most dangerous substances, more dangerous than some illegal drugs like marijuana and Ecstasy. The researchers, led by Professor David Nutt of Bristol University, consulted two groups of experts: psychiatrists with an expertise in addiction, and legal or police officials with scientific or medical expertise. The experts considered three factors to determine the harm associated with each drug—the physical harm to the user, the drug's potential for addiction, and the impact of each drug on society—and assigned scores to twenty different drugs. The researchers then calculated the drugs' overall rankings. Heroin and cocaine ranked most dangerous. Alcohol was the fifth-most harmful drug, and tobacco the ninth. Cannabis (marijuana) placed eleventh; Ecstasy placed near the bottom of the list. These findings are at odds with the current classification of dangerous substances in the UK and in most countries, where alcohol and tobacco are legal and cannabis and Ecstasy illegal.

The researchers assert that the current classification of drugs in the UK is "ill thought-out" and, "from a scientific perspective, arbitrary." They emphasize that tobacco causes 40 percent of all hospital illnesses, and alcohol causes more than 50percent of all visits to hospital emergency rooms. [The researchers therefore propose a new drug classification system, based on the actual risks **posed** to society—an "evidence-based classification of drugs."]
The researchers hope that the publication of their study will provoke debate about how drugs, including socially acceptable drugs like alcohol, should be regulated.

Activity A

Driving Me Up the Wall

With your classmate(s) discuss which of the following bad habits you find most annoying. Then discuss the questions that follow.

	Nail biting
	Chewing pens / pencils
	Pen twirling
	Doodling
	Smoking
	Nose picking
	Tapping one's fingers
	Jiggling one's leg(s)
	Chewing one's lip

	Being Lazy
	Interrupting people
	Picking scabs
	Gambling
	Eating junk food
	Spending too much money
	Drinking too much alcohol
	Spitting on the ground

1. Which of these bad habits are you guilty of? When did you start?
2. Have you overcome any of these bad habits? How?
3. Which of these habits do you think would be hardest to give up? Why?
4. Choose three of these habits and explain why people would get stuck on them.
5. What advice would you give to someone who was trying to:
   a. Stop smoking
   b. Stop gambling
   c. Stop eating junk food
   d. Stop drinking alcohol

Discussion

1. What are your worst habits? What bad habits have you **picked up** recently? Are you trying to **break these habits**?

2. Do you have any bad habits that bother other people?

3. Have you ever **made a conscious effort** to change something about yourself (i.e., overcome shyness, stop smoking)? What did you try to change? Were you successful in changing? Did it take a lot of **willpower**?

4. Do you think that you are **stuck on your habits** and **set in your ways**, or are you the kind of person who is willing to change?

5. Does your spouse / boyfriend / girlfriend have any bad habits that you have found difficult to adjust to? How about your ex-boyfriend / ex-girlfriend? How about your roommate(s)?

6. What are some of your good habits? What are some good habits that your boyfriend / girlfriend / spouse has?

7. What are some good habits that everyone should adopt?

8. What values (i.e., honesty, hard work, an appreciation of the arts) did your parents **engrain in you**?

9. How would you define an addiction?

10. In your opinion, what is the reason that people become addicted to the following?

a. gambling	b. shopping	c. cigarettes
d. chatting online	e. work	f. coffee
g. computer games	h. watching TV	i. cell phones

11. Are you addicted to any of these things? Are you worried that you can't **overcome** your addiction?

12. If there were no laws controlling things like gambling or smoking in public places do you think that people would be unable to control themselves?

13. How can you tell if someone is an alcoholic or a workaholic?

14. If everyone knows that cigarettes cause cancer and emphysema, why do so many people still smoke? Why does the government still allow cigarettes to be sold?

15. Why do some people become hooked on things, while others can try them a number of times and have no problems? Is there such a thing as **an addictive personality**? What are the characteristics of such people?

16. Do you know anyone who has **an addictive personality**? What kinds of things are they addicted to? Are they trying to change, or are you trying to change them?

17. Even doing healthy things, like exercising, can be taken too far. When does an interest in something become **an obsession**?

18. Have you ever **been obsessed with someone**? Looking back, why were you so **obsessed**? Do you think that love can be a kind of addiction?

19. Many people have certain "comfort foods" like ice cream or chocolate that they eat when they are depressed, agitated, or stressed out. Do you do this? What food(s) do you typically eat and how often do you eat them?

20. Which of the following quotes do you agree with more? Why?

    a. "Moderation is a fatal thing. Nothing succeeds like excess." -- Oscar Wilde

    b. "In everything the middle way is best: all things in excess bring trouble to men." -- Plautus

LESSON

14 Buying Beauty

Language Points

liposuction

He had a big tummy, so he had liposuction on his stomach.

nose surgery / nose reshaping / a nose job / rhinoplasty

She is thinking of getting a nose job because she thinks that the bridge of her nose is too low. But I think she looks fine.

beauty standards

Standards of beauty change over time. Women considered beautiful in Rubens' time would be considered overweight by today's beauty standards.

to feel insecure / to have insecurities / low self-esteem / an inferiority complex

She feels insecure about her appearance. She thinks that she is short, fat and unattractive.

alluring

Her full lips, long legs, slim waist and beautiful long hair are very alluring to men. Many men would love to go out with her.

unrealistic expectations

Some boys have unrealistic expectations about what their girlfriend should look like. They expect their girlfriend to look like a movie star.

to boost one's ego

Plastic surgery has really boosted her ego. Since the surgery, many people have said that she is beautiful. She feels much more confident now.

to be preoccupied with (something)

Many people are preoccupied with their appearance. They spend far too much time looking in the mirror and thinking about their appearance.

a botched job

It was a botched job. The surgeon must have made some mistakes during the surgery. She looks terrible.

a defect / misshapen

Ever since he broke his nose, it has not been a normal or natural shape. He wants to get a rhinoplasty to correct his misshapen nose.

Reading

There's no doubt about it: the modern world is becoming a cosmetic surgeon's paradise. Plastic surgery, which started in Beverly Hills and Palm Springs, California, has spread to Seoul, Tokyo, Beijing and Mumbai. Everyone seems to have a friend or relative who has had part of their body nipped, tucked, tweaked, lifted, Botoxed, or otherwise changed. Cosmetic surgery has become so common, in fact, that it is virtually a non-issue. Someone could announce that they were considering having cosmetic surgery with the same nonchalance with which they'd tell people they are going to the dentist, and no one would bat an eye.

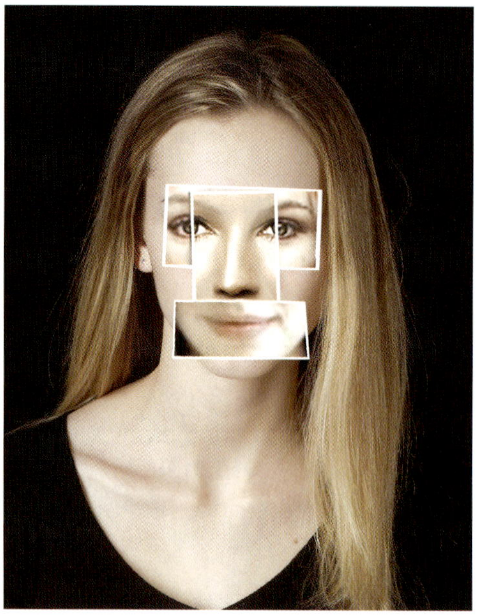

But who can blame the people, really? Who wouldn't want to look younger, thinner and prettier? A quick trip to the clinic and you can get rid of those extra kilograms on your lunch hour, have those heavy calves thinned, or get the same nose or jaw-line as your favorite celebrity? It can all be yours through the miracle of plastic surgery.

While cosmetic surgery has become popular the world over, the most common surgeries vary from country to country. Botox is the most requested cosmetic procedure in the U.S., Canada, Switzerland, Greece and Hong Kong. People in South Korea, Japan, Singapore and Russia request eyelid surgery most often. In Brazil and Germany, **liposuction** is the most common surgery. Women in Great Britain, Spain, Italy, Sweden, Finland, Norway and India opt for breast augmentation surgery more often than any other kind of cosmetic surgery. **Nose reshaping** is the most popular surgery in France and Taiwan.

Plastic surgeons claim that they do their best when they evaluate a **prospective** patient to see whether their perception of the likely results of surgery is realistic or if there is an **underlying** emotional problem behind the need for the surgery. Because of very **low self-esteem**, some individuals may have very **distorted** ideas about what they look like. They may **be** obsessively **preoccupied with** a perceived **defect** in their physical appearance even if others reassure them they look fine. However, since a plastic surgery clinic is a business like any other, it is unlikely that as many potential clients get refused as should be.

There are, however, some very good reasons to undergo plastic surgery. Some people want to look younger so they can get or keep a job. Appearance may not matter for a college professor or a scientist, but in certain jobs it does matter and plastic surgery can help. Others may have features that are unusually large or small, or **misshapen**, attracting unwanted attention and making them feel continually self-conscious.

Statistics indicate that the plastic surgery phenomenon exists in many countries, both eastern and western. In the US, 11.7 million cosmetic procedures were performed in 2007, a number that has increased 457 percent since 1997. In South Korea, by conservative estimates, 50 percent of women in their 20s have had some form of cosmetic surgery. And the number of men seeking to **boost their ego** is no less notable: 70 percent of men in a recent poll said that they would consider surgical improvements. People often say that getting cosmetic surgery will help them feel more confident about themselves. There are stories of women having surgery for the sole purpose of an interview, and some mothers even suggest that their daughters do so – all this, in the name of beauty.

Comprehension

1. Approximately what percent of women in your country have had some kind of cosmetic surgery? How many people do you know who have had cosmetic surgery of some kind? Do you know any guys who have had plastic surgery, or are thinking about it?

2. Would you consider having cosmetic surgery? If so, what would you change about yourself?
3. What kinds of cosmetic surgery are most popular? Why?
4. What do you think about people who have cosmetic surgery?
5. Do you think people who have cosmetic surgery are truly happier about themselves? Do they feel more confident?
6. Do you know of anyone who got plastic surgery done when it was not needed? What would prompt people to do this?
7. How would you feel if your spouse or partner wanted to have an expensive cosmetic surgery procedure? What would you do if you didn't actually agree that she/he needed it? What could she/he do instead? What procedures would you agree/not agree to?
8. What are the most serious side effects associated with plastic surgery procedures? Do you know of any 'botched jobs'?
9. Is it really possible to improve your self-esteem through cosmetic surgery or, does real self-esteem come from the inside?

Activity A

Made to Order

There are very few of us who look exactly the way we want to. If you had the money, and were so inclined, what would you change about yourself? On the list below, put a check next to the procedure(s) that you would most like to undergo. Then discuss the questions that follow with your classmate(s).

✔	Procedure (Technical Name)	Risk Factor	Us Average (2007, US $)
	liposuction	***	$5,350
	eyelid surgery	**	$2,840
	breast augmentation	***	$4,087
	breast reduction – women	**	$5,417
	breast reduction – men		$3,455
	buttock lift	**	$4,885
	calf reduction	**	$3,200
	chin augmentation	***	$2,254
	facelift	**	$6,792
	forehead lift	**	$3,337
	hair transplantation	*	$5,874
	lip augmentation	*	$1,611
	ear surgery (otoplasty)	*	$3,085
	nose surgery (rhinoplasty)	**	$4,357
	Botox injection	*	$380
	chemical skin peel	*	$718
	IPL laser treatment	*	$411
	laser skin resurfacing - ablative	*	$2,418

1. Which cosmetic surgery procedures did you choose? Why?
2. Some cosmetic surgery procedures have significant risks associated with them. What risks have you heard about?
3. Would you consider travelling to another country to get a better price or better quality assurance on any of the procedures you chose?
4. How do you think it would make you feel if you actually did have these procedures?
5. Do you know of anyone who has had any of the procedures listed in the chart? What procedures have they had? Were they satisfied with the results after the surgery?

(All figures from the American Society of Plastic Surgeons)

Activity B

You Can't Judge a Book by Its Cover

With your classmate(s) discuss what assumptions you would make about someone based upon each of the following characteristics.

Men	Women
• Balding	• Short hair
• Glasses	• Nose ring
• Acne	• Heavy make-up
• Dark skin tone	• Square jaw
• Overweight	• Big eyes
• Thin	• High nose bridge
• Long hair	• Overweight
• Earring(s)	• Light skin tone
• Casually dressed on a weekday	• No make-up

Discussion

1. Where do we get our perceptions of beauty?

2. What are today's **beauty standards**? How have hairstyles and fashions changed during the last 10 years?

3. Do you think that the cosmetics and fashion industry often overprice their products? If so, why do you think so many women are willing to pay the price?

4. Do you think that the cosmetics and fashion industry thrive by making women **feel insecure** about their appearance? How does it do so?

5. Women, far more so than men, are targeted by images of beautiful women in the media (on TV, in magazines, on billboards, etc.). Therefore, do you feel that the media play a part in women's insecurities?

6. Do you think that your feelings towards someone have an effect on how beautiful they appear to be? For example, as your liking for a member of the opposite sex increases, does he / she start to appear more beautiful to you?

7. "Sometimes it is the flaws in a person's face that give them their unique charm." Do you agree or disagree?

8. Why do you think that being thin is very fashionable these days, whereas several hundred years ago in Europe, it was fashionable to be fat?

9. Do you think that beautiful people receive too many unfair advantages? Can you think of some examples?

10. Do you think that beautiful people can improve their working environment and encourage people to work harder? Or do they just tend to make other people feel inferior and jealous?

11. When you find a member of the opposite sex physically attractive, what features do you notice?

12. Why do so many women's magazines have glossy ads featuring **alluring**, often scantily clad women? How does this work as an approach to marketing beauty products, perfume and clothing to women?

13. When you think of the women who are considered the most beautiful in your country these days, what do they have in common? How do modern ideals of beauty in your country compare to those of 30 years ago?

14. Do you think that the ideals of beauty around the world are becoming increasingly Western? If so, why is this occurring?

15. What do you think of the following quote? "There is nothing wrong with women's faces or bodies that social change won't cure; so the cosmetic surgeons depend for their income on warping female self-perception and multiplying female self-hatred." - Naomi Wolf

16. Who is the most beautiful person you can think of? What is it about this person that makes them so beautiful?

17. Is there such a thing as 'universal beauty' (i.e., characteristics that all cultures find beautiful)?

18. Very few women are happy with their appearance. Who do you think is responsible for women's negative self-image, men or women?

19. If your partner (girlfriend / boyfriend / spouse) had some physical feature that you didn't like, how would you tell him or her?

20. Do you think that all of the supermodels we see every day in the media give us **unrealistic expectations** about what women should look like?

21. If you could go in for **a cosmetic surgery procedure**, what would you like to have done? Would you worry about **the side effects** of the procedure?

22. Do you know anyone who has recently **undergone a cosmetic surgery procedure**? What did he / she have done? How does he / she feel about the results? What is your personal opinion? Were there any **negative side effects**?

23. Do you know of any cases of a botched job? Do the media report many cases of **botched jobs**?

LESSON

15 Stand Up for Yourself

Language Points

to stand up for oneself / to stand up to (someone) / to fail to stand up for oneself
He hit me, so I hit him back. I stood up for myself and stood up to him.

to get (straight) to the point / to come straight to the point / to get one's point across
I met my boss and got straight to the point. I told him that I wanted a raise.

to beat around the bush
Stop beating around the bush and tell me what the problem is.

to drop a few hints / to take a hint
I dropped several hints that I wasn't interested in dating him. I told him that I had a boyfriend, and I was too busy with my studies. But he didn't take the hint. Eventually I had to tell him the truth.

a pushover
He is a tough negotiator. He is certainly not a pushover.

to lose one's temper / to explode
I lost my temper and kicked the drink machine. I couldn't believe that it had stolen my money again.

to take advantage of someone / to be taken advantage of
I think she takes advantage of his good nature. She's always taking his money and having him run errands for her.

to let one's frustration build up
I allowed my frustration build up until I just exploded in anger one day.

to speak one's mind / to keep things to oneself
As I get older, I like to speak my mind because I think that it's important to let people know exactly what I think. But when I was younger, I used to keep things to myself.

to let someone walk all over you
Do you think I'll let you walk all over me? Well, I won't, ever!

Dialogue

A young woman bumps into a former classmate.

Martin: Oh! Hi there, Susan! Where **are** you **off to** in such a hurry?
Susan: Umm, nowhere...I was just...(sigh) Hi, Martin.
Martin: Wow, **fancy meeting you here of all places**! I mean, what a coincidence!
Susan: Yeah, it sure is. Actually, Martin, I was just about to...
Martin: Say, it's a good thing I ran into you. I've got two tickets to see the new James Bond movie, and I just couldn't find anyone to go with. How about it?
Susan: Well, Martin, you seem the thing is that I'm not really into James Bond movies.

Martin: Oh, really? But they're saying this is one of the best movies of the year. And Brosnan is up for an Oscar for his perfor mance.

Susan: Oh. Well, I can't argue with that. Um, what time does the movie start?

Martin: At 9.

Susan: Oh, that's too bad. I'm supposed to be meeting my mother at 8:30 to help her do the grocery shopping.

Martin: On a Friday night?! That's funny.

Susan: Well, it's the only time that I can help her.

Martin: Oh, I see. But, hold on a sec. What kind of grocery store is open on a Friday night at 8:30?

Susan: Listen, Martin, I tried to be polite about it, but you just couldn't **take the hint**. I'm not exactly sure how to put this, but I just don't want to go to the movies with you. I'm sorry.

Martin: Was it something I said?

Susan: No, Martin. Look, I should probably get going now.

Martin: No, seriously, tell me what I did wrong.

Susan: You didn't do anything wrong. It's just that **you're not really my type**.

Martin: What type is that?

Susan: Do I really have **to spell it out** for you? I'm not attracted to you.

Martin: Oh. But we could still go to the movie, you know, as friends.

Sue: Goodbye, Martin.

Martin: But I paid good money for these tickets!

Sue: Goodbye!

Comprehension

1. Have you ever been in this type of situation? How did you handle it?
2. In this type of situation, is it better to **tread softly** or **get straight to the point**?
3. Has anyone ever accused you of '**beating around the bush**'?
4. Are you usually worried about hurting other people's feelings?
5. Are you good at being assertive? If not, would you like to be?
6. Do you ever find it difficult to strike a balance between being pushy and being a pushover?
7. Have you ever met a person who just couldn't take a hint? How did you handle the situation?
8. On average, do you think that people in your country tend to be more direct than people from other countries? Try to give some examples.

9. Are there certain situations in which people from your country tend to be indirect and others in which they are more direct? Give some examples to support your opinion

10. Are there some people you find it especially hard to be direct with? How about people who are noticeably older than you?

Activity A

Striking a Balance

There is a fine line between getting your point across and winding up in a conflict. Read through the situations on the left and, for each of the possible responses on the right, discuss the likely outcome. Which do you think would have the desired effect? Which would be ignored? Which would get you into trouble? Which would you be most likely to say?

Situation	Possible responses
You are at a restaurant that you've eaten at several times before and everything has been fine, but this time your food takes a long time and is cold when it finally does come. You call the waiter over and say,	1 "I am sorry to trouble you, but don't you think this food could be a little on the hotter side?" 2 "If you came to my house for dinner, would you expect to have to wait an hour to eat cold soup?" 3 "Look, excuse me, not only is this food late, but it's also ice cold. I don't think that's acceptable. Do you?"
Two of your colleagues in the section next to yours have been flirting with each other regularly for the past two weeks and disrupting everyone else in the office. You've asked them to keep it down once already, but they don't seem **to be able to restrain themselves**. So one day, you say,	1 "Look, is it too much to ask that the two of you have a little consideration for the rest of us?" 2 "In case you hadn't noticed, some of us are actually trying to do some work around here. You should try it sometime; if you're not too busy, that is." 3 "Uh, hello? I just thought you might like to know that everyone can hear what you are saying, so you might want to keep it down a little."
You're a housewife. The light bulb in your hallway has been burnt out for four months, and your spouse has been promising to fix it for quite a while, but hasn't got around to it, despite your nagging. You lose your patience and say,	1 "I'm **sick and tired of asking** you to replace this damn light bulb. Is it really too much to ask?" 2 "I'm sorry, but what is it exactly that is stopping you from fixing it?" 3 "I don't mean to nag, but if you're not doing anything, is there any chance that you could fix this?"

Your boss is always burdening you with extra work when other people could take care of it just as well. This has meant you've had to give up having drinks with your friends five Fridays in a row. You've had enough. You build up the courage one night to say,	❶ "Alright, just this once more, but after this, you've got to find someone else." ❷ "Surely there's someone else you could ask for a change." ❸ "So, let me get this straight. You are asking me to waste yet another evening here? Are you for real?"

Activity B

Let 'Em Have It

When you find yourself in a touchy situation, it's sometimes hard to keep from losing your temper and dealing with the problem aggressively. Many times, though, using strong language or exhibiting rude behaviour can be counterproductive and just make matters worse. Knowing how to express complaints effectively can help resolve them quicker.

In each of the following situations, someone has been inconvenienced or somehow treated unfairly. With your classmate(s), take turns expressing complaints about the situations. Try to be firm and assertive, but not rude. Your classmate(s) should try to offer a good excuse for their behavior. If you feel that their explanation is reasonable, you can let them off the hook. If not, you can really let them have it! After each scenario, discuss whether you think your classmates handled the situation tactfully, rudely, or feebly.

1. You're at the movies and the person behind you keeps bumping or kicking your chair.
2. You're at one of your favourite restaurants, but the service is very slow and when the food arrives at your table, it's cold.
3. You are at the department store and are having trouble finding what you're looking for. The only sales person in sight is busy having a private conversation on the phone.
4. Your friend borrows a considerable amount of money from you. A month has passed since you had agreed he or she would pay you back, and still no money!
5. You had agreed to meet your classmate yesterday. You waited for over an hour, but he / she never showed up. It seems like he / she just completely forgot about it.

6. You lent your car to your classmate, but when it was returned to you, the gas tank was empty, there were muddy footprints all over the upholstery, and the interior smelled funny and was littered with garbage.
7. You have left several messages on your classmate's answering machine, and have even sent him / her an email, but you've had no reply.
8. Your classmate is your neighbour, and his / her dog has been doing its business right outside your front door. It has happened twice before, but you've had enough!
9. You went out drinking with your classmate last night. He / she drank far too much and behaved terribly, embarrassing you in front of your other friends.
10. You are waiting to get on the elevator and your classmate brusquely steps in line in front of you.
11. Your classmate is always arriving for class late, sometimes as much as 20 minutes into the class. You find it really disruptive and want him / her to try harder to be on time.
12. On several occasions, your classmate has interrupted you while you have been speaking in class.

Discussion

1. Do you consider yourself to be a naturally **assertive** person? Do you ever wish that you were more or less assertive?
2. Do you tend to respect people more if they are assertive rather than easy-going? Why or why not? If you act assertively, do you think that other people will respect you more?
3. If a person is easy-going, do you think that they tend to **be taken advantage** of by others?
4. Do you think that it is necessary for women to be more assertive than men? Justify your view.
5. Is it true that **assertiveness** is seen as a desirable quality in men but undesirable in women? Is it possible for women to be assertive and feminine at the same time?
6. Is there a difference between being 'nice' and being 'a **pushover**'? How could you define this difference?
7. Do you agree with the saying '**nice guys finish last**'? Can you think of any exceptions to this?
8. Do you sometimes find it difficult to **strike a balance** between being easy-going and being assertive?
9. When someone asks you to do them a favor, do you find it difficult to say no?
10. A person who **stands up for himself/herself** in a Western working environment generally tends to be respected. Is this also true in your country?
11. In a situation where you are unhappy with something, do you find it easy to complain? Do you usually complain immediately, or do you **let your frustration build up** until you finally **explode**?
12. Do you tend to act more assertively in front of some people than others? Can you think of some examples?

13. If you have a different opinion to an older or more senior person, do you tend to **speak your mind** or **keep your thoughts to yourself**?
14. Do you think that it is necessary to be assertive to be successful in business? How about in your private life?
15. Did you ever **let somebody walk all over you** and regret it later? What happened?
16. In a touchy situation, is it usually better to **come straight to the point** or **drop a few** hints first?
17. Some people are easy to manipulate. Have you ever **taken advantage of** another person's good nature to suit your own purposes?
18. What is the difference between being assertive and being a jerk?
19. Some people fail to stand up for themselves even when they stand to lose a lot. What do you think it is that they are afraid of?
20. These days, assertiveness courses are becoming popular. Do you think that it is possible to change our basic nature and become more assertive simply by attending a course?
21. In your country, do men tend to become more assertive as they become older? How about women?

LESSON

16 Too Good to Be True

Language Points

a little far-fetched
His excuse was a little too far-fetched for me to believe.

to be / get ripped off / a rip-off / to rip someone off
Eric's ticket cost much less than ours. I think we've been ripped off! $300 for these tickets? What a rip-off !

to be skeptical (of something)
I'm very skeptical. I think he might be lying.

a convincing liar
I'm not a convincing liar. That's why I always tell the truth.

to see (right) through (someone/a lie)
He told me that he had been at the office working. But I saw right through his lie immediately.

to be taken in (by something) / gullible
I can't believe you were taken in by that advertisement promising that taking those pills would help you lose weight. You are so gullible.

a compulsive liar
I think he's a compulsive liar. Sometimes he appears to believe that he is telling the truth.

a polygraph test / a lie detector / a lie detector test
His lawyers announced that he had taken and passed a polygraph test. They say that the results prove that he is innocent.

to bend the truth
I sometimes bend the truth when I don't want people to know the real facts.

to be upfront (with someone) (about something)
He's very upfront about why he wants the job: he'd like to earn a lot more money.

Honesty is the best policy.
I have always believed that honesty is the best policy, so I am going to tell her the truth.

Dialogue

Two neighbors meet in a parking lot of a local auto repair shop.

John: Hey, Arnie!

Arnold: Oh, hi John. **Fancy meeting you here**. What are you doing? **Getting the car tuned up**?

John: No. It's a long story. I brought the car here two weeks ago to **have the radiator replaced**.

Arnold: Yeah...and?

John:	When I came to pick it up, it turned out that several other things had been repaired.
Arnold:	Well, that's good.
John:	Not really. The thing is I **wasn't contacted** about any of it. But they just went ahead and fixed it all even though I hadn't **given them the go-ahead**.
Arnold:	Oh. Well, that isn't good.
John:	No, not at all. And what's more, the bill was out of this world! And the craziest part was the radiator hadn't even been replaced. That was the reason I brought the car in in the first place! Unbelievable, eh?
Arnold:	Yeah, geez... So what did you do?
John:	I blew up at the manager. He was pretty good about it, though. He said he'd make his mechanics replace my rad and that they'd give me all the other repairs they'd done at cost. So, in the end it worked out alright. But I certainly won't be letting them do any more work on my car, that's for sure.
Arnold:	Hmm. I'm glad you told me about that. I was just about to bring my car in for a tune up. I think I'll take it over to Joe's Garage. He's pretty reliable, although he charges a bit more than other places.
John:	Good plan. I'd better get going. See you later, Arnie.

Comprehension

1. Can you think of any examples of **false advertising**, where the description of the goods or services offered failed to meet your expectations? What did you do?

2. Have you ever **been ripped off** by anyone (e.g. a mechanic, a doctor etc)? Explain what happened.

3. In your country, which companies (or industries) are notorious for false advertising and **ripping people off**? Are there any companies that you are particularly **skeptical of**?

4. If you feel that someone has **ripped you off**, do you usually complain to them about it or just let it go?

5. Do you consider yourself to be **shrewd** when it comes to getting a good deal? Can you usually spot which products and services are **a rip-off** before you make a purchase?

6. Do you think that there is ever any justification for **cheating someone**? Have you ever **ripped someone off**?

7. Isn't a certain amount of lying, or at least exaggeration, to be expected in advertising?

8. Does your country have strict laws about false advertising? Does the law usually favor the seller or the customer?

9. Do you feel that some big name products are **a rip-off**, or are you happy **to pay for the name**?

10. Some ads on television seem **a little far-fetched**. Have you seen any ads lately that seemed a bit **too good to be true**?

11. Westerners often feel pride when they get a good deal. Is it the same in your country? Or do some people feel pride when they spend a lot of money on something?

12. Although there are laws protecting the public from dishonest businesses, Western countries rely heavily on the principle of 'caveat emptor' (which means 'let the buyer beware'). Do you think that the responsibility should be on the customer to protect themselves?

Reading

IT is widely known that people who tell lies usually experience psychological strain, unease or agitation because of the worry that their lies may be detected. Other physiological reactions include excessive blinking, stammering, sweating, shaking, avoiding eye contact, shortness of breath and changes in the tone of voice, to name only a few.

During his testimony to the grand jury regarding the sex scandal involving White House intern Monica Lewinsky, President Bill Clinton touched his nose an average of 26 times a minute. As with former President Clinton, sometimes when an individual is lying, he tends to exhibit nervous habits. Some experts watch for these signs to detect whether a person is being truthful or not.

A more scientific method for detecting whether a person is lying or not was developed in 1920. A polygraph, or 'lie detector' (as it is more commonly known), can detect changes in breathing patterns, pulse and blood pressure that typically indicate, with about 90 percent accuracy, that someone is nervous about something they are trying to conceal.

However, this machine is incapable of measuring physiological rates in persons who exhibit diatheses, a condition that enables a person to lie and show minimal physiological changes. To combat this problem, scientists are now perfecting a machine that measures electrical impulses in brain waves. Some people believe this new device may be capable of detecting even the most convincing liars, even those individuals who exhibit diatheses.

Comprehension

1. How good are you at lying? Are you **a convincing liar**, or can people **see right through you**?

2. Can you usually tell that someone is lying? If so, how?

3. When you lie, do you exhibit any nervous reactions (such as those mentioned in the article)?

4. Have you ever **been taken in by someone**? How long was it before you eventually found out the truth?

5. Do you agree with the expression, "Honesty is always the best policy."? If not, when do you think it is better to lie?

6. Is it possible to go through life without ever telling a lie (even a 'white lie')? Would living in this way have a positive or negative effect on your relationships?

7. Do you think that famous people and those in positions of authority have a greater responsibility to set a good example by not lying?

8. Politicians are well known for lying. Do you think that politics encourages lying and corruption?

9. Some people are **compulsive liars**. Do you think that it is possible for a person to lie so much that they are no longer aware that they are lying?

10. Do you think that **polygraph testing** is a reliable way to detect lies? Explain your answer.

11. If the police asked you to take **a lie detector test** to prove that you were innocent of a crime, would you agree?

12. Do you think that a machine (even one designed to measure brain activity) will ever be able to detect lies with 100% accuracy? Why, or why not?

Activity A

Typical Excuses

One very common occasion for lying is when people need to come up with excuses to explain their mistakes or irresponsibility. With your classmate(s) take turns giving typical excuses for each of the types of people in the list below.

Example:
Students who do poorly in school
"The teacher was boring." "The books weren't interesting." "The class was too early." "That's not my area of interest." "I lost my notes."

1. People who smoke
2. People who are late for school or work
3. People who are late for a date
4. Men and women who have love affairs
5. Parents who spank their children
6. Husbands who beat their wives
7. Drunk drivers
8. People who have messy houses
9. Drivers who speed
10. Students who give up trying to learn English
11. Public officials who take bribes
12. People who steal
13. Singles who want to stay single

Activity B

Truth or Lie

Read over the ten questions below and select which five you will respond to honestly and which five that you will lie about, indicating this in the first column of the table. Conceal this from your partner(s). Think about the lies that you will tell beforehand so that you won't have to hesitate and thereby reveal the lie. During the conversation, observe your partner carefully and ask a maximum of two follow-up questions to try to uncover their deceptions. Mark down which of their answers you think were lies. After the conversation, reveal to each other which answers were in fact lies. Then discuss the questions that follow.

Your Answer		Question	Your Partner's Answer		
Honest?			Honest?		Correct?
No	Yes		No	Yes	
		1. Have you ever cheated on an important test?			
		2. Can you talk about the most embarrassing thing that has ever happened to you?			
		3. Can you describe your worst dating experience?			

		4. Do you have any bad habits?			
		5. Do you ever pick your nose?			
		6. Have you ever gotten really drunk?			
		7. What is the worst thing you've ever said behind someone's back?			
		8. Have you ever been dumped by someone?			
		9. Have you ever had a crush on any of your teachers?			
		10. Is there any item of clothing that you are embarrassed to admit you wore when you were younger?			

1. When you guessed correctly that your partner was lying, what gave him or her away?
2. When you were lying to your partner, did you find it difficult to keep a straight face?
3. Are you usually a convincing liar? Does it depend on whom you are lying to?
4. Is there a person who always knows when you are lying?
5. Is it sometimes necessary to lie in order to save face?

Useful expressions

Making statements

- I know this is hard to believe, but…
- You may not believe this, but…
- Believe it or not…
- It's completely / 100 percent true.
- Don't you believe it?
- I'm not kidding / joking.
- I'm not joshing you.
- Would you believe it?

Expressing skepticism

- Do you (really) expect me to believe that?
- That can't possibly be true.
- There's no way you could have…
- I think you're giving me a line about…
- I don't believe a word of it.
- You have to be kidding.
- Don't make me laugh.
- Get serious! / Get real!
- Get out! / Get out of here! / Get out of town!
- You're full of it.

Activity C

White Lies

Read through the following list of lies. Can you explain them? When would you hear them? Have you ever heard any of them before? Answer the related questions below.

TOP TEN LIES

10 You don't look a day over 40!
9 I'll pay you back right away.
8 I'll do it in a minute.
7 I can't remember.
6 Your hair looks great!
5 I won't tell anyone!
4 Trust me.
3 That was delicious.
2 Don't worry...you can't really notice it.
1 I love you!

Questions

1. Which of the above lies do you consider a white lie?
2. Which of the above lies have you told someone?
3. When was the last time you used one of them? Who did you lie to?
4. Which of the above lies do you use the most? What other lies have you used?
5. Can white lies be harmful sometimes? If so, when?
6. Do you generally trust people?
7. Do you consider yourself to be gullible or are you usually skeptical about what people say to you?
8. How do you know when someone is lying to you? What tips you off that people are lying to you?
9. Do you think that not telling someone something is just as bad as lying to them?

Discussion

1. When was the last time you told a lie? (Remember: white lies are still lies.)
2. What's the biggest lie you've ever told?
3. Have you ever told a big lie to someone you love?

4. How often do you mislead (or lie to) your parents, your boyfriend or girlfriend, your husband or wife?

5. Are you generally **up front with** people, or do you tend to **bend the truth** a little?

6. Are you a good liar? What makes a person a good liar?

7. When was the last time you got caught telling a lie? What were you lying about? How did you get caught? What happened?

8. How do you feel when you have been untruthful to people? Have you ever felt really guilty about telling a lie?

9. Can you usually tell if someone is lying to you? What signs do you look for?

10. What is the biggest lie you've ever been told? What did you do when you found out the person had lied to you?

11. Have you ever been deceived by somebody you really trusted?

12. Have you ever lost a friendship because of a big lie?

13. What people do you trust the most?

14. Is honesty always the best policy? Can you think of a situation in which it would be okay to lie? Explain your answer.

15. Should husbands and wives always be completely honest with each other? How about boyfriends and girlfriends?

16. Is there anyone in your life now that you are completely honest with?

17. If you had a chance to give your girlfriend / boyfriend / husband / wife / best friend a **lie detector test**, what questions would you ask them?

18. Who do you think lies more often: men or women? What kinds of lies do men tell? What kinds of lies do women tell?

19. Who are better liars: men or women? What makes them better liars?

20. What would you think of having lie detector equipment in the workplace or in schools? Would it be acceptable? What rules should govern the use of such equipment?

21. Would you submit to a polygraph test in order to be considered for a job?

22. Are there any jobs in which it is an advantage to be a good liar?

LESSON

17 In a Perfect World...

Language Points

to raise the bar

The arrival of many excellent new students at our school will definitely raise the bar. Academic standards will definitely be high higher.

a perfectionist / perfectionism / to achieve perfection

She is such a perfectionist that even the tiniest mistake bothers her.

to have / set realistic, attainable goals

Perfection is not an attainable goal.

to have / set excessively high and unrealistic goals / a pipe dream / pie in the sky / far-fetched

He usually sets excessively high goals. They will never be anything more than a pipe dream.

perfect in every respect/way

My vacation was perfect in every respect. The weather was sunny and warm. The beach was beautiful. The food was delicious. The service in the hotel was great.

to have high expectations

I have high expectations for myself. I expect a great job and a great salary, a healthy life, and a great wife.

a soul mate

My girlfriend and I are soul mates. We are perfectly suited for each other and have similar attitudes, values and beliefs.

high ideals / idealistic

When he graduated from university he had very high ideals. He was always honest, principled and generous, and he expected everyone else to be the same.

pet peeve

My pet peeve is slow drivers in the fast lane. Passengers in my car always tell me not to worry, that it's only a minor annoyance, but it really annoys me.

Reading

Raising the Bar

We are all trained from birth to strive to achieve positive results in almost everything we undertake. When people aim at reaching **excessively high and unrealistic goals**, it is often mistakenly seen in our society as desirable or even necessary for success. However, recent studies have shown that **perfectionist** attitudes can both rob us of our sense of personal satisfaction and actually interfere with success.

Perfectionists often learn early in life that other people value them because of how much they accomplish or achieve. They base their self-esteem primarily on external

standards, leaving them vulnerable and excessively sensitive to the opinions and criticism of others. To defend against this, they may try **to achieve perfection**.

There are a number of mental habits that perfectionists typically develop. They often equate failure to achieve their goals with a lack of personal worth or value and may become very fearful of failure. Perfectionists also worry that, if they let others see their flaws, they will no longer be accepted. Trying to be perfect is a way of trying to protect themselves from criticism, rejection, and disapproval. Worst of all, perfectionists may demand the same standards of others, thereby frustrating others and alienating themselves.

Healthy goal setting is quite different from the self-defeating ways of thinking associated with **perfectionism**. **Realistic goals** are normally related to an individual's wants rather than to external expectations. Their goals are usually **realistic**, internal and potentially attainable. Therefore they tend to enjoy the task at hand rather than focusing only on the end result. When they experience disapproval or failure, their reactions are generally limited to specific situations rather than generalized to their entire self worth.

The first step out of perfectionism is simply to realize that it is an unhealthy and undesirable illusion, compared to realistic, **attainable goals**. There are alternative ways to think that are more beneficial. Not only are you likely to achieve more without your perfectionism, but you will feel better about yourself in the process.

Comprehension

1. After reading this article, would you say that you are a **perfectionist**?
2. Do you feel as if what you accomplish is never quite good enough?
3. Talk about some of the goals you've set for yourself in your life. Are they **realistic and attainable**?
4. Do you feel you must give more than 100 percent on everything you do or else you will be **mediocre** or even a failure?
5. Talk about some of the goals you've set for yourself in your life. Are they realistic?
6. What is more important to you, the process or the goal?
7. When you make a mistake in front of others, how does it make you feel?
8. What are some positive things that can only be learned by making mistakes?

9. Think of a mistake you have made recently and talk about all the things you can learn from it.

10. Do you often do things to impress others? Who? Why?

Activity A

All that Glitters Is Not Gold

Most people imagine how wonderful life would be if only they were rich, famous, and beautiful. However, very few of us stop to consider that even people who have lives that are very enviable might have serious problems to deal with. Although we tend to idealize them, wealth, fame and beauty are probably burdens in some way.

With your classmate(s), brainstorm as many downsides to each of the following situations as you can think of. Afterwards, share some of your more creative ideas with the class.

Being incredibly rich	Having a very attractive spouse
Being world-famous	Being highly intelligent
Living to be over 100	Being very self-confident
Being very popular	Being able to read people's minds
Having a very expensive car	Being able to predict the future
Living in a huge house	Being the president of a large company

Activity B

An Imperfect World

What drives you crazy? What do you hate? What are your pet peeves? There are all kinds of things that get under our skin. Some things are minor annoyances and there is little we can do to change them. However, some problems are more serious, and we need to know how to express our complaints clearly.

What are some of your pet peeves about the following?

- restaurants
- public transportation
- English class
- your parents / siblings
- celebrities
- shopping
- vacations
- the Internet
- your office / university
- society
- movies
- politicians / politics
- television
- children
- your boyfriend / girlfriend
- telephones
- teenagers
- habits
- pets
- photos

Activity C

Island

At some time or other, we find our minds wandering as we start to imagine a perfect place to live - a place where every day would be like a holiday and we wouldn't have a care in the world! However, if you really had the chance to construct your own utopian society, how would you go about it?

Imagine you and a group of similarly minded people have decided to buy a small island in the Sound Pacific on which to establish your very own self-governing country. You and your classmate(s) have been elected the decision-making commitee. Consider each of the categories and decide how best to handle them.

1. Science and technology
2. Government
3. Distribution of possessions and wealth
4. Transportation
5. Education
6. Crime and punishment
7. Buildings and architecture

Discussion A

Imagining a Perfect Life

1. If your life were **perfect in every respect**, what would it look like?
2. What would you no longer be doing if your life were **perfect in every way**?
3. If you could live anywhere in the world, where would you choose to live, and why?
4. If money were no object, what kind of place would you like to live in? Describe your dream house / apartment.
5. If you had everything that you could possibly want, what would you have?
6. If you could design your ideal lifestyle, what would it look like?
7. If you could design your ideal career, what would it be?
8. Describe your perfect girlfriend / boyfriend / husband / wife.
9. If you could go back in time and change some aspect of your childhood or school experience, what would you change and why?
10. What is the one main thing that you would like to change about your own personality in order to improve your life? Is it something that you have the power to change? If so, how? If not, how cold you compensate for it?
11. What habits do you think you have to break in order to achieve greater success?
12. Do you **have high expectations** for yourself? Did your parents always have high expectations for you?
13. People often complain about other's faults. If you could change something about someone you know, whom would you change and what would you change about them?

Discussion B

In a Perfect World...

1. Do you think that it is possible to be completely content with your life? Do you know anyone who is perfectly content with his or her life?
2. If you could make five positive changes to the society that you live in, what would they be?
3. In what way do you think that a person's quality of life has an impact on his/her health?
4. What do you think about the quality of life in your hometown compared to other cities in the world? Which aspects are better and which are worse?
5. Do you think it is possible to have a perfect society (utopia), or does the nature of human beings make this impossible?
6. Can you remember a day that was **perfect in every respect**? What happened?
7. Does our quality of life depend simply on our living environment, or is it more related to positive thinking?
8. People often think that they will be happy when they achieve a certain goal in life. However, this is rarely true. Why do you think that many people are never satisfied with their life? Are you easily satisfied?
9. "Nothing has a stronger influence psychologically on their environment and especially on their children than the unlived life of the parent." (Carl Jung, 1875-1961). How can parents' **high expectations** of their children be damaging?
10. Do you believe that everybody has a **soul mate**? Can finding a perfect partner really make our lives happy?
11. The attempt to implement a perfect political system (e.g., communism) has failed in many countries in which it has been tried. Why do you think communism failed?
12. Is having **high ideals** a good or bad thing? Why do you think so?
13. Perfectionists tend to be very hard on themselves. Can you think of some ways that making mistakes can be beneficial?
14. Sometimes we have dreams that we just can't seem to achieve. Is it better to admit that we're beaten and 'give in gracefully' or to 'die trying'?
15. Is some dissatisfaction with our lives a positive thing? Is this what keeps us growing and trying to improve ourselves?

LESSON

18 Nose to the Grindstone

Language Points

to keep (one's) nose to the grindstone

If I keep my nose to the grindstone, I will be able to finish this project before the deadline.

to take the initiative

When there's a problem, he's always the first person to act. The managers love how he always takes the initiative.

to receive (some kind of) recognition

I'm glad that he got the promotion and raise. He has finally received recognition for the excellent work that he has done.

to be (fairly) rewarded/compensated

I did so much extra work. I don't think I was compensated fairly. I think I deserved much more than I received. I should have received a big bonus.

to suck up to (someone) / to brown nose

He always sucks up to the boss because he wants a promotion and a raise.

to sell yourself (to other people)

When I have an interview, I always try to sell myself to the interviewer. I present a really polished image, and I talk about all of my good points.

to be (stuck) in a rut

After ten years in the same job with the same manager in the same building, he was in a rut. He was tired of always following the same routine.

to manage one's time / to organize one's time / to keep track of time

I usually have to work on several projects at the same time, so I have to organize my time very carefully and keep track of how I spend my time.

a contingency / a glitch

There was a computer glitch while I was making my presentation. I had no contingency plan, so I had to reschedule the presentation for next week. I felt like a fool.

Dialogue

Two friends smoking in the stairwell are chatting about work.

Hank: Hey, Frank. Uh...You look a little down today. Is something wrong?

Frank: Um...Not really. I'm just concerned about my job interview next week.

Hank: Oh, I didn't even know you were looking for a new job.

Frank: Well, I don't feel I'm getting anywhere in my present position.

Hank: I know what you mean. I feel the same way sometimes.

Frank: You know, I've got a family now, so I have to think very carefully about the future. What would you do if you were in my shoes?

Hank: Well, let me see...Umm... Have you tried talking to your manager?

Frank: No, not really. He isn't very - how should I put this - approachable. And besides, shouldn't he be able to see for himself that I'm a good employee? Shouldn't he be the one to approach me? What would you do if you were me?

Hank: I'd have to think about that... Well, for starters, you could ask your manager out for coffee. Try to find out how he feels about your work. Uh...tell him how your projects are progressing. You could mention that you've learned a lot in your present job and you feel that you are ready for a new challenge.

Frank: What! Are you nuts! I've never had coffee with him before!

Hank: Look, Frank, how should I put this... If you don't **take the initiative** to strut your stuff, nobody else will. You have to have more confidence in yourself and what you do.

Frank: You're right. I guess I've never given myself credit for the things I've accomplished around here.

Hank: That's right! You're a good employee, Frank, so go for it.

Comprehension

1. When you work hard at a job or on a project, how important is it to **receive some kind of recognition**? If you fail to receive the recognition you feel that you deserve, how do you react?

2. If you were in a similar situation to Frank, how would you have handled it?

3. At companies in your country, are individuals' efforts usually **fairly rewarded**? Which kind of reward would you prefer: a pay raise, a big bonus, a promotion, or a better benefits package?

4. Is **sucking up to the boss** a good way to get noticed in a company? If not, what are other ways to get noticed?

5. Do you find it easy to approach senior people such as your boss or teacher? If you were unhappy about something, would you usually confront the person directly or try to avoid the problem like Frank?

6. What do you think are the qualities of a good manager?

7. Are you good at **selling yourself to other people**? If you were trying to **get a promotion** at work, what would you list as your strong points?

8. Have you ever been '**stuck in a rut**' in a job or situation where you felt that you couldn't progress any further? How did you eventually get out of the situation?

9. If a job or situation doesn't seem to be progressing the way you'd like it to, do you usually try to persevere, or do you simply try to get out as fast as possible?

10. If you had a problem at work, would you tend to confide in other workers or keep the problem to yourself? What are the pros and cons of each approach?

Reading

Men Motivated by Colleagues' Income

A recent experiment provides scientific evidence that men in the workplace are motivated not only by the size of their salaries, but also by how much money they make relative to coworkers. The researchers—economists and brain scientists at the University of Bonn—tested 38 male participants in pairs, having them perform tasks and promising payment for the successful completion of each task. The participants lied down next to each other in parallel brain scanners and performed the same task simultaneously. If a participant solved the task correctly, he received a financial reward, anywhere from 30 to 120 euros. Each participant also learned how his partner had performed and how much money he had received.

Throughout the experiment, the researchers used the brain scanners to monitor changes in blood flow to the ventral striatum, the part of the brain which is activated when someone feels strong motivation. The researchers found that activity in the ventral striatum increased when a participant completed his task correctly and subsided when he was unsuccessful. However, the most significant finding was the influence of the performance of the participant in the other scanner. Activation was highest for participants who got the right answer while the other participant got it wrong. Researchers also analyzed cases in which both participants completed the task correctly. When the participants received the same payment, there was only moderate activity in the ventral striatum. However, in cases where both participants successfully completed the task but were awarded different amounts of money, blood flow increased significantly for the participant receiving the larger sum but decreased for the participant receiving the smaller sum. The experiment revealed significantly more brain activity with men who knew they were earning more pay than their rivals.

The experiment contradicts traditional economic theory, which holds that men are only interested in the absolute size of their salaries. Rather, the study reveals that men are very concerned with their peers' salaries and are strongly motivated by competition. Next on the agenda for the researchers is an experiment to determine if the same is true for women. Moreover, the research team has planned experiments with Asians, which will provide some insight into the influence of cultural factors in competitive thinking.

Discussion

1. The researchers have planned experiments with women and Asian participants. What results do you expect from these experiments? Will women and Asians be mostly concerned with their own performance and the absolute size of their payment? Or will they, like the German men who took part in the first experiment, be strongly motivated by the payment received by their colleagues?
2. What motivates you in the workplace? Rate each on a scale from 1 (totally unimportant) to 10 (critically important) and discuss your ratings with a partner.
   - Earning a name for yourself in the company and winning the respect of your colleagues for the quality of your work?
   - The absolute size of your salary?
   - Earning a higher salary than your colleagues.
   - Earning a promotion?
   - Pleasing your manager/boss?
3. In your life, are you strongly motivated by the pursuit of money?
4. Do you care about your colleagues' salaries?
5. Would you work harder or more productively if you knew your colleagues' salaries?
6. Do you often think about your paycheck and wish you earned more money? If yes, why is a high salary so important to you? Also, what do you plan to do to increase your salary?
7. Do you think knowledge of colleagues' salaries would bring a healthy competitiveness to workplaces and increase productivity? Or would it create jealousy and unhealthy rivalries between workers and destroy workplace harmony?
8. Should companies and schools introduce a system that creates more competition between employees and rewards the best and most productive employees with a higher salary?

Activity A

Time Management

Take a look at the quadrant chart below and discuss the questions that follow with your classmate(s).

	URGENT	NOT URGENT
IMPORTANT	PANIC I'm normally: • in crisis • stressed out • procrastinating • inefficient	QUALITY I'm normally: • on task • productive • reliable • organized
NOT IMPORTANT	DECEPTION I'm normally: • unfocused • easily distracted • non-productive • "busy"	WASTE I'm normally: • wasting time • doing nothing • lost • making excuses

1. When you think of the way you spend most of your time each day, which of the above 'quadrants' would you say best describes your attitude towards work? Why is this?
2. Overall, how would you rate yourself in terms of your efficiency at doing work? What are your strengths and weaknesses with regard to **managing your time**?
3. Do you work better on your own, or as a member of a team?
4. When working with other people, do you focus on the work that you can do best?
5. Do you give yourself enough time to complete tasks or projects?
6. Do you **tackle** the most difficult pieces of work first?
7. Do you keep your workspace neat and organized?
8. How do you **keep track of your work deadlines** and the degree of importance of each item?
9. How do you organize your time each day? Do you set aside time each day for: (1) checking and responding to email messages, (2) planning, (3) doing your work, (4) taking breaks?
10. How extensively do you schedule your time? Do you allow for '**contingency time**', to accommodate emergencies and **glitches?**
11. Do you make decisions about what to do first based on what's most important to your **over-arching goals**, or based on who's complaining the loudest?
12. Do you agree to every project or task that your supervisors ask you to do, or do you ever refuse to take on work that you know you cannot complete without significant stress?
13. Do you get enough sleep and keep yourself healthy? What effect do you think this has on your ability to stay organized and perform at work?
14. What would you say is the biggest interruption or distraction for you? How could you eliminate this to enable you to work uninterrupted for longer periods of time?
15. Do you work best "under pressure", when you have **a tight deadline**, or when you are given enough time to work steadily and calmly? Why?

Activity B

Go with the Flow

With your classmate(s), choose one of the following topics to discuss. You can support or oppose the following statements.

- The workweek should be four days long.
- Workers should be able to go home after their **shift** is over without feeling guilty.
- Making hiring decisions on the basis of age or appearance should be illegal.
- The **dress code** at most companies should be a lot more flexible.
- Messenger, and similar programs, should be banned in offices.
- Managers should be more open to input from lower level employees.

Each time you take a turn speaking, you will make your point, designate the next person to speak, and give them one of the following phrases to start their statement with. Try to give your classmate(s) a different expression each time. The important point is that you should not stop talking at all.

In addition,...	However,...	In my opinion,...
Furthermore,...	Nevertheless,...	For example,...
On the other hand,...	Well, I feel that...	You may have a point, but...

Here is an example of what you will be doing;

Jim: **In my opinion**, the dress code at work should be a lot more flexible. Why should I have to wear dress pants and a dress shirt and tie at work?

Kate: **Well, I feel** that a dress code promotes a professional atmosphere. And what if clients come to the office? Company employees need to present themselves as professionally as possible, so they need to dress professionally.

Jim: I see what you're saying, but I feel that I can do my work just as well in casual clothes than in a shirt and tie. Actually, if I'm dressed casually, I will feel more comfortable. And if I feel comfortable, I can work more productively.

Kate: **You may have a point, but**...

Remember it is important not to stop talking.

Activity C

Mismanagement Styles

Read the descriptions of the managers below and then discuss the questions that follow with your classmate(s).

Name:	Richard Stockwell	Herbert T. Spencer	Wilma de Koonig
Nickname:	Dictator Dick	Hectic Herb	Wishy-washy Wilma
Attitude towards Employees:	"A certain amount of fear **does wonders for productivity.**"	"You can always **squeeze more out of them.**"	"They're a great bunch of guys. We really **gel together**. We're just one big happy family."

Richard Stockwell

Herbert T. Spencer

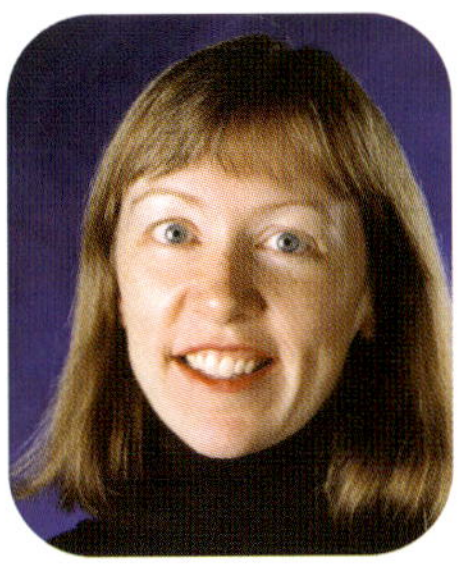

Wilma de Koonig

Work Ethic:	A demanding, uncompromising manager who routinely yells at and humiliates employees.	A disorganized man who always sets unrealistic goals without consulting employees	An understanding, **people-oriented manager** who tends to focus on the group dynamics rather than the task at hand
Famous Saying:	"Teamwork is a lot of people doing what I say."	"I need this yesterday." "Doing it right is no excuse for not meeting deadlines."	"Okay, no problem." "We can always be a little flexible." "I'm okay, you're okay."
Employees Say:	"Don't let him see me talking to you!"	"What a moron! He always expects us to drop everything and jump into **crisis mode** because of his oversights and bad planning."	"It's no secret that Wilma can't **handle any conflict**. Last week, she **broke into tears** in a meeting."
Productivity:	The most-producive department in the company ten years running	This department has yet to meet any of its targets	Upper management is thinking of phasing out her department.
Other Features:	The highest **turnover** of employees in the company **ten years running**	Employees in this department commonly ask for transfers, complaining of **unrealistic workloads** and high stress levels	Everyone loves her, but no one takes her seriously.

1. Which of these managers would be the worst one to work for? Why?
2. Do you now have (or have you ever had) a manager or boss who resembles any of these managers?
3. What are the pros and cons of the management styles that each of the managers above have adopted?
4. What are the qualities of a good manager?
5. Have you ever had a boss or manager who you admired? What was he or she like?
6. If you were a manager, how would you act? Would you rather be a manager or an employee? Why?

Discussion

General questions about working environment, work ethics, work culture, etc.

1. In some countries workers change jobs often and easily, but in others most employees stay in the same job for life. Which system does your country have? Is it in the process of changing? What are the pros and cons of each system?

2. When was the last economic crisis or recession in your country? Did it have any long-term effect on workers' work ethic?

3. Look at the table presented below. Does the average employee in your country work longer hours than the average employee in foreign countries?

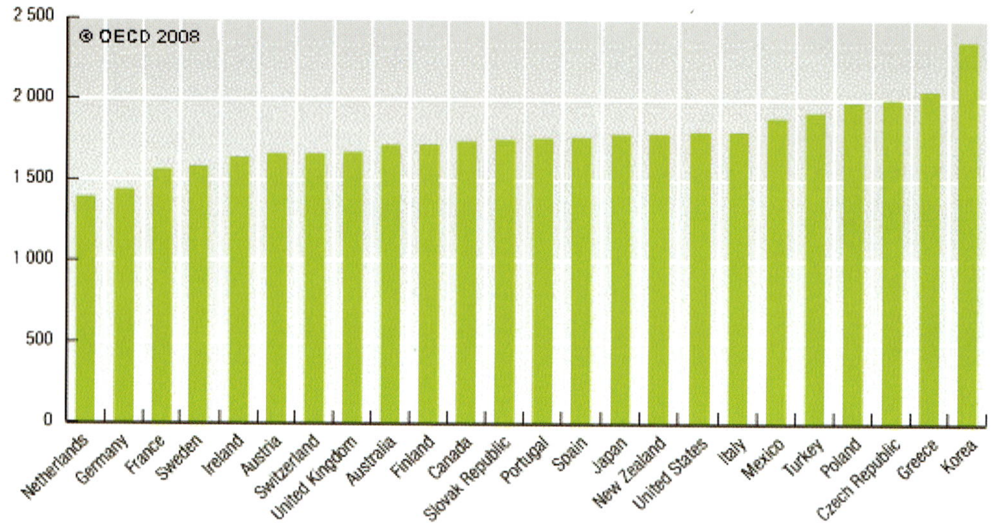

4. In almost every country in Europe, employees receive four weeks of holidays per year, and in the US, 12 days is the norm. What about your country? How many paid vacation days do most employees receive? Do you think that the average employee's holiday entitlement is sufficient? If not, how much paid holiday per year do you think is reasonable?

5. Do you think that individual companies should be allowed to decide the length of their working week? Or should all companies be required by law to limit their work weeks to five days?

6. As your country becomes richer, do people still work as hard as before? Are they working the same hours per week? Or are they becoming interested in hobbies and other diversions as the economy develops and workers have more **discretionary income** (income available for spending after paying taxes and buying the essentials, such as food, clothing and housing)?

7. How much money do you need to make to fulfill you dreams and desires?

8. In your opinion, have women made great strides in the workplace in recent years? Is there still sexual discrimination at work? Are women now treated equally to men in the workplace? If not, do you think that this will ever happen? Why or why not?

9. Who among the people you know has the most interesting job? What is it?

Questions for those who are not currently working

1. Do you think it is more important to make a lot of money or to enjoy your job? If you had to choose a satisfying job or a well-paying one, which would you choose? Why?

2. What job would you like to have in five years time? In ten years time? What is your long-term career goal?

3. What would be your dream job? Do you think it would be possible for you to get this job?

4. If money weren't a problem for you, which job would you prefer to have?

5. Would you like a job in which you traveled a lot?

6. Would you like to work in a foreign country? Which country? For how long? What would be the pros and cons of working abroad?

Questions for those who are currently working

1. Do you like your job? What do you like most about your job? What do you hate the most?

2. Are you happy with the career you have chosen? Or would you like to change to a different career? If you want to begin a new career, what will you need to do to make the change?

3. What three adjectives would you use to describe yourself as a worker? How would your co-workers describe you? Would you consider yourself to be an ambitious person at work? Would you describe yourself as a workaholic?

4. Do you like your boss? Why or why not? What are good skills for a boss? Does your boss have them?

5. Do you have any enemies at work?

6. Are you a manager? Would you like to have a management position? What are the pros and cons of being a manager?

7. Do you think your company is well-run?

8. In your opinion, do people at your company generally work productively during work hours? Or is there a lot of wasted time?

9. Are **tight deadlines** common at your workplace? Do you feel that it creates a lot of unnecessary stress? What are the consequences if you miss a deadline? Have you ever missed one?

10. Do you (or anyone you know) work for a multinational company? What are the pros and cons of working at a multinational? Would you like to work for one?

11. In your opinion, is it necessary to go out drinking regularly with the boss and other employees? Does it generate a good working atmosphere? Are there any disadvantages?

12. In your office environment, are employees discouraged from questioning management decisions? Is it the same at most companies in your country? When employees are discouraged from **questioning management decisions**, are mistakes more likely to go unchecked?

13. Do you know anyone who really **sucks up to the boss**? Has it helped them get a promotion?

14. At what age would you like to retire? What do you think you will do after you retire?

15. Have you ever thought of starting your own business? If so, what kind of business would you start, and why? Would you be happier if you were self-employed?

LESSON

19 Get Your Kit On

Language Points

to go AWOL / to be absent without a leave
He went AWOL during the war, so when he was found he received a punishment.

barracks / mess hall
After a long day of training, I went to the mess hall for dinner, then to my barracks to get some rest.

rank
He rose to through the ranks – from Private to Sergeant to Lieutenant.

to build character
Some people believe that military service builds character. Men who have experienced military service are often much stronger psychologically than those who have not.

to toughen (someone) up
His father sent him to boxing school to toughen him up. He is now much better able to handle physical hardship.

superiors
He always had to obey orders from his superiors.

a draft dodger
During the Vietnam War, many young Americans were draft dodgers. They avoided compulsory military service even though they were obligated by law to join.

a pacifist
He is a pacifist. He believes that war and violence are always wrong. That's why he is trying to avoid military service.

to prove oneself in combat
He proved himself in combat during the war. All of the other soldiers in his military company could see that he fought bravely and effectively.

Reading

A young man has written the following letter to one of his friends.

February 12, 2003
Dear Mark,

How are things with you? I hope you're all settled in at law school and getting down to some hard work - quite a change from your time teaching here in Korea, I bet. (Just kidding.) Even though I know you enjoyed yourself here, I'm sure it was still really nice to get back home to America.

Wow, I feel a bit funny writing a letter. It must be at least five or six years since I last wrote anyone a letter by hand. In case you wondered, I'm writing you a letter because I won't have a chance to send you an email or call you for a few months. I started my Korean military service six weeks ago. Ugh! It's no picnic. I've been here less than two months and I'm already plotting to **go AWOL** at the first opportunity!

I'm serving in the Air Force as a military police officer. It might sound exciting to you, but let me assure you - it isn't at all. Basically, my job entails standing at the gates and checking all the traffic into and out of the air base. We work in four-hour shifts, with eight hours' rest. After four hours standing without a break, my legs and back are just killing me. When I work the night shift, it's so boring I feel like I'm going to go crazy. And the cold is terrible, especially at night. The uniforms we have to wear have almost no insulation.

I share the **barracks** with thirty-five other young men, and we share one small bathroom. Most nights we talk about women, and a few of the guys have told me that it's pretty common for guys to get dumped in their first year of military service when their girlfriends find someone else.

The worst thing about being here is the food. In the **mess hall**, we have to line up with 500 other soldiers for what seems like forever. And when we finally get our food, it's just terrible. What's worse, because of our low **rank**, we are forced to eat everything we're given. Do I ever miss my mom's cooking!

Anyways, if the last few weeks are any indication, things look pretty bleak for the next twenty-six months. There are some good guys here. We play soccer every night, come rain or shine, and I think that's what's going to get me through this hell. I keep telling myself that it's good for me and that it's going to **build character** and **toughen me up**, but right now it just sucks. You should be thankful that, as an American, you don't have compulsory military service. You wouldn't last a day.

Well, I'm thinking of the good times we had in L.A., and all the crazy stuff we did when you were here last year. That keeps me going, too.

Counting the days,

Jin

Reading Questions

1. What do you think of Jin's description of life in the army? Does it sound unbearable? Does it seem realistic?
2. Jin is describing his life in the Air Force. What have you heard about other divisions of the military (i.e., the Navy, the Marines, Special Ops, the Regular Army)?
3. Do you have more respect for people who have served in the military? Are some divisions of the military considered more honourable than others?
4. Jin writes that he has made friends with some of his fellow soldiers. Do men form strong friendships with people they meet in the military?
5. What forms of discipline are employed to correct misbehaviour in the Korean military?
6. How common is mistreatment or abuse of **lower ranks** by their **superiors**?
7. Do men commonly pick up any bad habits in the military, such as smoking, drinking, or swearing?

8. Jin mentions that the men in his squad play a lot of soccer. What other activities do soldiers do to pass the time?
9. Becoming a member of the military usually involves undergoing some sort of initiation or hazing. What sorts of this thing happen in the army?
10. If life in the military is as dreadful as Jin describes, why do some people make the decision to make their career in the military?

Activity A

Military Service - For Better or Worse

It is said that a man undergoes many changes from the time he goes into the military to the time when he comes out again. Discuss each of the following changes with your partner and say which ones you agree or disagree with and why.

Men...

1. are more ready to settle down when they come out of the military.
2. are more disciplined and careful after military service.
3. are better at doing household chores after military service.
4. have more respect for authority and are more law-abiding after military service.
5. are more responsible and realistic when they come out of the military.
6. are more violent after they have completed their military service.
7. have more conservative social and political views after military service.
8. have more energy and enthusiasm for life after military service.

Activity B

Draft Dodger

Take a look at the following excuses for getting out of military service and say whether you think they are valid or not and why.

1. My father is the chairman of a conglomerate. He needs me to take over the business because he is retiring.
2. I've spent most of my life eating junk food and playing computer games. Unfortunately, I didn't pass the army physical!
3. After beating up a couple of guys with a baseball bat, I was sent to see a shrink. His report said that I was unstable and prone to violence.
4. My girlfriend is about to have our baby and there is no one else to take care of them except me.

5. I accidentally shot myself in the foot when I was younger. Now, if I even see a gun, I feel sick and start trembling.

6. I've heard that privates in the army are forced to smoke by senior officers. I'm a non-smoker and I don't want to get lung cancer.

7. I am a pacifist, and my religion forbids all forms of violence.

Activity C

Get Your Kit On!

For a long time there has been a debate as to whether or not women should be allowed in combat. As equality between the sexes continues to increase, military combat is one of the few remaining roles that excludes women. Below are three women's opinions regarding females in combat. Say which you agree with most and why. Then answer the follow-up questions.

1 We've come a long way towards achieving sexual equality during the last couple of decades. Women have proven themselves in almost every field. Do we really want to take a step backwards? Although I do not want to enter into combat myself, I would argue for any woman's right to do so, including my own daughter's.

2 I've been through all aspects of military training and have passed everything from physical strength and fitness to advanced weapons training with top grades. And besides, military combat these days relies more on high-tech hardware, expertise and quick thinking than on brute strength. I'm just as capable as any of the guys, so why shouldn't I have a chance to **prove myself in combat** and, if necessary, die for the country I love?

3 On the one hand, I've always been brought up to believe that women can do anything they want to. On the other hand, women do not belong next to men on the battlefield. Whether we like it or not, we have to face the fact that women are simply not as well equipped physically to survive in battle as men are. It's bad enough that young men should be slaughtered in battle. Why should countless women be expected to do the same simply in the name of equality?

Questions

1. Do you think that women are better able to survive on today's high-tech battlefield than they would have been in the past?

2. If your wife or daughter wanted to go into battle, would you try to dissuade her? Why or why not?

3. Do you think that it is just a matter of time before women are allowed into battle?

4. Do you think that most male soldiers would be less willing to fight or kill enemy female soldiers than they would enemy male soldiers?

5. Should the government make military service compulsory for women as well as men? Why or why not?

Discussion

1. Do you think that the duration of mandatory military service is appropriate? Why or why not?
2. Many people think that military service completely changes a person. Do you agree with this, and if so, are the changes for the better or worse?
3. Do you know someone who seemed to have changed after completing his or her military service. What changes did you notice?
4. Do you agree that military service can teach a person discipline, **build their character**, and teach them respect for society?
5. In some countries, women currently serve in the army. Do you think that there is a place for women in today's high-tech army? In these days of greater equality, should women also be expected to do mandatory military service?
6. Do most people receive good treatment during their mandatory military service? What is the worst altercation you've heard about, been involved with, or witnessed?
7. Soldiers only get paid a pitifully small amount of money during their mandatory military service. Do you think this amount is sufficient? Why or why not?
8. Many men try to avoid mandatory military service. Is army life too strict, or are there other reasons?
9. Some rich or famous men are able to avoid military service. Do you think that such people should be allowed to get out of their duty? Why or why not?
10. Male university students often have to interrupt their studies for a couple of years while they are in the military. What are the reasons for this? Wouldn't it make more sense to get it out of the way before entering university?
11. Do you think that having mandatory military service is simply a cheap way of maintaining a certain number of soldiers in the army at all times? If all soldiers were professional, it'd cost the government a lot of money. Are young people being taken advantage of? Should this be changed?
12. Instead of getting rid of mandatory military service completely, can you think of some ways to improve the system?
13. Would you consider the military as a career choice? Why or why not?

LESSON

20 The Price of Fame

Language Points

to capture one's imagination

Every four years, the FIFA soccer World Cup of captures the imagination of millions of people around the world.

to be publicly disgraced

He was publicly disgraced after he was arrested.

to hound (someone)

The movie made her famous. But ever since then, the press has hounded her.

to be endorsed

The company paid $2 million to the movie star to have their new aftershave endorsed. He says he uses it and likes it.

evasive

He was asked about the rumor that he has a new girlfriend, but his answer was very evasive. So now the rumor is even stronger.

the price of fame

Because there are so many paparazzi in the world, giving up your privacy is often the price of fame.

gossip column

The gossip columns of several newspapers published stories about the famous couple's breakup.

attention seeker / attention-seeking behavior

He no longer makes great movies, so he tries to stay famous by engaging in attention-seeking behavior.

to rise to fame

He rose to fame in the 1990s as the star of a popular TV program. Since then, he has starred in several movies.

world-famous

The movie was extremely popular around the world, and the leading actress became world-famous.

Dialogue

An reporter from MovieFile.com is interviewing Jeremy Price, a recent Oscar nominee, for a real-time on-line chat.

Movie File:	Jeremy Price has been nominated for an Oscar for his role in Eugene Steven's adaptation of The Taming of the Shrew. His sudden rise to fame has caught the attention of both movie reviewers and fans alike. He has kindly offered to chat with us today from his home in West London. Mr. Price, hello!
Jeremy Price:	Hello.
Movie File:	I saw 'The Shrew' just yesterday. Your performance was **spellbinding**. How did you prepare for the role?

Jeremy Price: The same way that I always prepare - with a hot bath and a bottle of Scotch!

Movie File: Ha ha.

Jeremy Price: No, only joking, of course, I actually did a lot of research into the part and studied videos of other memorable performances and tried to take the best aspects of each and add my own unique style into the mix. I'm glad you liked it!

Movie File: Any plans for **a sequel** yet?

Jeremy Price: Well, I don't know about that but I have recently been offered the chance to play the part of the **arch villain** in the next 007 movie!

Movie File: Looking forward to that. Our listeners out there in 'cyber-land' are curious, I'm sure, about the recent rumours that you've started seeing Melanie Cruickshank, who **starred opposite you**. How is that going?

Jeremy Price: Well, actually I prefer to **keep business and pleasure separate**, so we never used our tongues when we kissed **on the set**!

Movie File: Hmm. Fair enough. But **there are rumours circulating** that Mel's former boyfriend was the director, Eugene Steven. How did the tension **on the set** contribute to the success of the movie?

Jeremy Price: It just meant that I did the opposite of everything he said!

Movie File: As **a relative newcomer**, what do you think about the veteran actors and some of the more outrageous things they do?

Jeremy Price: Hey, you think they're outrageous, you ain't seen nothin' yet!

Movie File: Well, actually, some of our sources have told us that Steven sent you back to your trailer to sober up on more than one occasion. Do you have a problem handling your liquor?

Jeremy Price: Yeah, I do admit to having a bit of a drinking problem: two hands and only one mouth!

Movie File: Do you think that your womanizing and your drinking problems will ever interfere with your career?

Jeremy Price: Well, I try to encourage women to interfere with me at every opportunity and, as for the drink; a few stiff scotches always give me a clearer perspective on things.

Movie File: Ha ha. What's it like being you? What do you do on an average day?

Jeremy Price: Well, after having my usual salmon and poached egg for breakfast I read the Times. After that I usually take a walk to clear my head after the hangover from the night before. It also helps to give me some inspiration. The rest of the morning is spent relaxing with my Jack Russell and **reading over my lines**. Then it's off to work until the evening. It's usually about the time that I stagger back home after yet another show biz party that I consider checking into Alcoholics Anonymous, but I'm always too drunk to make the call!

Movie File: Ha ha. Sounds like a pretty relaxed lifestyle! What would you be doing if you weren't acting?

Jeremy Price:	Well, it's funny you should ask, but I've heard that there is one job that's even more relaxed than this. So, I sometimes think about giving it all up to go and be an English teacher somewhere in Asia.
Movie File:	Somehow I can picture you doing that. It's quite similar to acting in many ways. Anyways, that's about all we have time for today.
Jeremy Price:	Great, well lovely to talk to you old chap, can I interest you in a scotch sometime?
Movie File:	I hope we do get the chance. All the best with your career! If the start is any indication, we look forward to great things. Thanks for taking the time to talk with us. Bye.
Jeremy Price:	Bye!

Comprehension

1. Do you envy Jeremy Price? Is there anything about his lifestyle that sounds appealing?
2. Do you think that his life is really as relaxed as he makes it sound? What do you think a typical celebrity's lifestyle is like?
3. If you were asked some of the questions the interviewer asks Price, would you feel that your privacy was being invaded?
4. What do you think of the way Price handles these questions?
5. Do you think that fame changes people significantly? In what ways?
6. What is it about the lives of famous people that **captures our imagination** so much?
7. Every day, you can see news about famous people's private lives all over the news. Are you interested in such stories? Why or why not?
8. Do you think that most people have a fascination with seeing the famous and powerful **publicly disgraced**? Why is this?
9. Name one famous person and list three questions that you would love to ask him or her.
10. In the US and Europe, the paparazzi is notorious for **hounding celebrities**? Do you think that the paparazzi go too far in pursuing pictures of celebrities and stories about their private lives? Is there a paparazzi in your country?
11. If you were a celebrity, how would you react to people asking you about your private life? Would you be honest, be **evasive**, or get aggressive? Why?

Activity A

People You Love to Hate

Say which famous person you would most like to... and why.

1 ··· be like?

2 ··· meet and talk to?

3 ··· spend a romantic weekend with?

4 ··· see publicly humiliated?

5 ··· not see anymore?

6 ··· entertain you and your friends?

7 ··· be marooned on a desert island with?

8 ··· read gossip about?

9 ··· spy on?

10 ··· go on a trip with?

Activity B

Wannabe

We are all influenced, to some extent, by famous people whether we'd like to admit it or not. Sometimes they can encourage us to buy a certain product or adopt a certain style. In other cases, they can influence the way we act or motivate us to achieve particular goals. For each of the following categories, discuss the ways in which your favorite celebrities influence you.

a	Buying particular brand name clothing worn by your favorite celebrities
b	Buying brand name products **endorsed** by your favorite celebrities in advertisements.
c	Using the same establishments and services used by your favorite celebrities (e.g. restaurants, health facilities, etc)
d	Watching films which star your favorite actors
e	Hairstyles
f	Style of dress
g	Reading books by your favorite author
h	Listening to music and attending concerts by your favorite musicians
i	Reading newspapers and magazines with gossip about your favorite celebrities
j	Adopting the lifestyles and hobbies of celebrities you admire

Activity C

Quotations about Fame and Gossip

Match the lines to make quotations about fame and gossip. In pairs, compare your answers, then discuss the meaning of each quotation. Which do you agree and disagree with?

1. " It is not necessary to be rich and famous to be happy.	**A.** there would not be four friends in the world."-Elaise Pascal
2. " Be nice to people on your way up because	**B.** It is only necessary to be rich." - Alan Alda
3. " Whenever a friend succeeds,	**C.** is when you gossip about them."- William Penn
4. " There is only one thing worse that being talked about,	**D.** you'll meet them on your way down."-Wilson Mizner
5. " Being a star	**E.** praise her to her girlfriends." -Benjamin Franklin
6. " Whoever gossips to you	**F.** small minds discuss people." -Eleanor Roosevelt
7. " Great minds discuss ideas; average minds discuss events;	**G.** and that is not being talked about." scar Wilde, -Oscar Wilde
8. " The only time people dislike gossip	**H.** a little something in me dies." -Gore Vidal
9. " If everyone knew what others said about him,	**I.** will gossip about you." - Spanish proverb
10. " To find out a girl's faults,	**J.** was never as much fun as dreaming of being one." -Marilyn Monroe

Discussion

1. Have you met many famous people? Describe a memorable experience you had.
2. In your home country, do you think that people's interest in celebrities and appetite for news about them is increasing these days?
3. Do you ever **get sick of** seeing the same old faces on television or in the magazines? Who are you getting sick of these days?
4. Is there such a thing as overexposure, or is it a case of 'the more the better'? Say why you think so.
5. Who is your favorite celebrity? What is it you like about them? Have you ever seen them in person?
6. Do you think that many celebrities are over-paid compared to people with important jobs such as teachers, doctors, and aid-workers?
7. What do you see as the pros and cons of being famous?
8. Should celebrities expect to have some privacy, or is that **the price of fame**?
9. Do you like to read the **gossip columns**? Do you believe everything you read about celebrities?
10. Why do you think that so many people are interested in the lives of celebrities?
11. Does everyone have at least some small desire to be famous?
12. If you could be famous, what would you like to be famous for?
13. Some celebrities are addicted to fame, and they become depressed if they lose it. Are such people just **attention seekers**?
14. Do you have a role model? Who is it and what is it that you admire about them?
15. If a celebrity that you like is advertising a product, do you think that you are more likely to buy that product? Why or why not?
16. Some people **rise to fame** quickly. What type of problems do you think that they face?
17. Andy Warhol famously said, "In the future, everyone will be **world-famous** for 15 minutes". How about you? ; have you ever experienced fame? If so, for how long? Explain what happened.
18. Do famous people really **make any worthwhile contribution** to our lives? Explain your answer.
19. How would you react if you saw your favorite actor or actress sitting alone in a coffee shop?

20. Which newspapers, magazines, and websites publish stories about celebrity scandals in your country? What scandals are in the news currently?

21. How do you think you would feel if you were a celebrity and you read a false story about yourself?

22. How do you think it would feel to live as a famous person?

23. Does the public have a right to know about the private lives of famous people?

24. "You don't need talent to make it in the world of entertainment (dramas, pop music, etc.): just good looks and a good manager." Do you agree or disagree?

Appendix - Grammar and Usage

2 Notes Usage: I Will Crush You

The word 'crush' has several meanings, and can be used both as a verb and as a noun. 'To crush someone' can mean to overwhelmingly defeat them in games, battles, or sports.

- Korea **crushed** Canada in a soccer game.

'To crush someone/ something' can also mean to smash an object or person.

- It is a good idea **to crush empty cans** before throwing them in the trash.

Understanding these possible meanings, you may be able to understand the confusion that native speakers feel when they hear Konglish expressions like the following.

× She crushed on him in high school. (Huh?!)

'A crush" (noun) is used in a romantic sense to mean a short-term infatuation with someone. It is normally used with the verb 'have', and the preposition 'on', as follows.

- She **had a crush on** him in high school.

3 Notes Usage: Get Your Head Around This!

You may want to express the idea that other people you know share your views about what is right and wrong. You may be tempted to say something like the following.

× No one around me thinks so.

This may be interpreted to mean 'no one physically present'(around me). Even more confusing would be the phrase;

× No one surrounding me thinks so.

This means 'no one encircling me'. In this context, most native speakers would say something like

- **Nobody I know** thinks so.
- **None of my friends or family** think so.
- **I don't know anybody who** thinks so.

4 Grammar Focus: Time Is On My Side

Nouns can be classified as either countable (ex. car, duck or piece) or uncountable (ex. water, money or peace) nouns. However, some nouns have BOTH a countable and an uncountable form. The word "time" is such a word, as can be witnessed in the following examples:

- Sherry has seen that movie several times.[countable]
- Mike spends a lot of time in the gym.[uncountable]

In the first sentence, the countable noun "times" refers to different and separate situations. In the second, the uncountable noun "time" refers to the time we measure in hours, minutes, and seconds.

7 Notes Usage: It's up to You!

Sometimes students are confused about whether to use the expression 'it's up to...', or 'it depends on...', so it is not uncommon to hear sentences like the following.

× I really want to go to the beach, but it's up to the weather.

'It's up to... ' is more limited in how it can be used. Whereas 'it depends on...' can be used with a person or a thing as an object, 'it's up to...' can only be used with a person as an object. For example;

Why don't we go camping this weekend?

× It is up to the weather.
- It is up to you.
- It depends on the weather.
- It depends on you.

8 Grammar Focus: You Should Have Figured This Out By Now.

It can be difficult to use the prepositions 'by' and 'until'. It might be easier if you kept in mind the fact that '**by**' means '**at that time or before**' and '**until**' means '**at that time or later**'. Consider these examples:

- Our professor said we have to finish our essays **by** Friday.
  (on or before Friday)
- Traffic is so bad today that we won't get there **until** ten.
  (at ten or later)

9 Notes Usage: Dressed to Kill

When you go to a department store you'll probably notice different areas designated 'Men's Wear,' 'Ladies' Wear,' etc. However it is NOT common for native speakers to use "wear" as a noun in everyday speech.

× I like your **wear**.

Instead, you can use 'wear' as a verb in a noun clause, as follows.

- I like **what you are wearing**.

Or you can use a more specific expression.

- I like **your outfit**.
- I like **your suit/ dress/ pants/ etc.**.

Similarly, if you think that someone usually dresses very nicely, don't use an expression like 'way of wearing'.

× I like her way of wearing.

Better expressions are:

- I like **the way she dresses**.
- **She has good taste in clothes.**
- **She's very stylish.**
- **She's a sharp dresser.**

10 Grammar Focus: I Want You To Get This Right

× My parents want that I go to America next year.

In English, it is not grammatically correct to say you "want that someone does something". When the object is an action, the verb 'want' is followed by a to-infinitive. For example:

- I want to take an English conversation class again next month.
- She wants to eat another piece of cake!

In the above example, the speaker is talking about what she herself wants. But when we talk about wanting someone else to do something, we can use the following form; 'want someone to do something'. So,

× His parents want that he studies English very hard.

should be

- His parents want him to study very hard.

10 Grammar Focus: The causative

The causative is a common structure in English. It is used when one thing or person causes another thing or person to do something. In conversation, we often use the causative form when we want to talk about having some kind of service performed for us. This lesson will explain how causatives are formed, and how to use them.

For example, consider the difference in meaning between the following sentences.

- I cut my hair last night. (I did it. It was pretty difficult!)
- I had my hair cut last night. (The hair dresser did it.)

There are two verbs commonly used in causative structures; 'have' and 'get'. The following sentences have the same meaning.

- I had my hair cut last night.
- I got my hair cut last night.

Basic causative structures
There are two basic causative structures; active and passive.

Active

Subject	Causative verb	Agent	Action verb	Object
I	had	two kids	wash	my car.
We	had	professionals	paint	our house.

Passive

Subject	Causative verb	Object	Past participle		Agent
I	had	my car	washed	by	two kids.
We	had	our house	painted	by	professionals.

As with other passive forms, if the agent is obvious, unimportant, or unknown, it can be left out.

I	had	my car	washed.
We	had	our house	painted.

Other Causative Verbs
'Let' and 'make' are two other causative verbs that are commonly used. 'Let' is used to mean 'allow' or 'permit'. 'Make' is used to mean 'force' or 'compel'.

- We don't usually let our son eat snacks between meals.
- My boss made me get coffee for everyone at the meeting.

The verb 'let' does not have a passive form. 'Make' has a passive form, but it is extremely uncommon and usually only seen in formal writing.

11 Notes Usage: You Will Learn This in Five Minutes

You may want to tell your classmates some stories about your travel experiences. When doing so, you will more than likely need to use some sort of time clauses to let them know when your trip happened and to make sure that they understand the sequence of events in your story. Be careful when using time clauses like 'in', 'later', 'before', and 'ago', as they are often confusing for students. Unfortunately, they are extremely common words in English.

One important concept to keep in mind is the idea of 'point of reference', which refers to the point in time from which the speaker 'measures' other points in time.

- I will be going to Guam in two months.

In the above sentence, the point of reference is the time of speaking. If the speaker said this on April 1st, she means to say that she will be traveling to Guam on June 1st. But if the speaker was only going to stay in Guam for two weeks, and then return to Korea, she would say.

- I will be coming back two weeks later.

Here the point of reference is not the moment of speaking, but two months into the future.

Likewise, we use 'ago' to talk about some point in the past, if the point of reference is the moment of speaking, but 'before', or 'earlier' if the point of reference is not the moment of speaking.

- I went to Hawaii three years ago.
- My wife and I had gone on vacation there 10 years before. (13 years ago)

13 Notes Usage: Talking 'bout my Generation.

You might want to refer to people of a particular generation when talking about this topic. For instance, you might want to say that people aged 18-30 are especially likely to become addicted to the Internet, whereas older people aren't. Remember that the word 'generation' always refers to a group of people, so to refer to one person as 'a generation' is wrong. 'Generations' are also relative to how old both the speaker and listener are, so it is common to use the comparative adjectives 'younger' and 'older'.

So, one should not say;

× You are a young generation, so you are interested in the Internet.

Instead you should say;

- You are young, so you're interested in the Internet.
- You're part of the younger generation, so...
- You're a member of the younger generation, so...

Likewise, it's wrong to refer to a group of people who are about the same age as 'generations'. So, it's wrong to say;

× Young generations like on-line games.

Instead, you ought to refer to a group of people who are about the same age as a 'generation' (singular).

- The younger generation likes hip-hop music."

Or you can avoid the problem altogether.

- Young people like on-line games.

14 Notes Usage: We Can't Allow This Mistake.

You might want to say that using marijuana isn't or shouldn't be allowed in Korea. There are several verbs in English that can be used to express that some action is or isn't allowed. You might be tempted to use the verb 'admit', but this would not be correct.

× Street drugs shouldn't be admitted.

Although 'admit' can be used in this sense in a courtroom, it is normally used to mean that someone is or isn't allowed to enter some place.

- If you don't have a ticket you won't be admitted.

The other (and probably more common) meaning of "admit" (verb) is to confess that you did something wrong.

- I admit that I've tried marijuana once or twice, but I didn't inhale.

Better verbs to use in this context are 'permit' or 'allow'.

- I think that no one should be permitted to use street drugs for any reason.
- Using soft drugs is allowed in some countries. I think that Korea should follow

15 Notes Usage: I Don't Like the Looks of That

Avoid using the word "looking" as a noun. For example, we don't say that we 'like someone's looking'.

× We didn't like his looking.

Instead, we use the following sorts of expressions.

- We didn't like the way he looked.
- We didn't like his appearance.

Likewise, we don't say that someone 'has a neat/ clean/ good looking'

× He had a good looking.
× At a job interview you should have clean and neat looking.

Rather, use expressions like the following.

- He was good-looking.
- He had a good appearance.
- At a job interview you should have clean and neat appearance.

16 Notes Usage: A Penny for your Thoughts

One way we can 'soften' a criticism that we need to make is to explain to the listener that it is only our own personal opinion. You should be careful about what sorts of expressions you use to say this. Korean students of English often use words like 'mind', 'thinking' or 'thought' when they mean 'opinion'.

For example, don't say:

× That is just my thinking/ thought/ mind.

You should say:

- That's just my opinion.
- That's just what I think.

Instead of saying;

- What's your mind?
- How do you think?

You should use a different expression, like;

- What do you think?
- Do you agree?
- What's your opinion?
- What are your thoughts about?

17 Notes Usage: Why Can't You Get This Right?

If you notice that some problem seems to be occurring and you wish to inquire about the situation, be careful about using forms like:

- What's the matter with you?
- What's wrong with you?
- What's your problem?

The personal pronoun forms "you" and "your" make it sound like the person you are talking to is causing the problem (ex. "What's your problem? Are you crazy? How could you do that?"). Usually, it's a better idea to use one of these forms:

- What's the matter?
- What's wrong?
- What's the problem?

SLE 3B Textbook Recordings

Track	Title
1	Introduction and Lesson 1 - Dialogue
2	Lesson 2 - Dialogue
3	Lesson 3 - Dialogue
4	Lesson 4 - Reading
5	Lesson 5 - Reading
6	Lesson 5 - Dialogue
7	Lesson 6 - Dialogue
8	Lesson 7 - Dialogue
9	Lesson 7 - Reading
10	Lesson 8 - Reading
11	Lesson 9 - Dialogue
12	Lesson 10 - Dialogue
13	Lesson 11 - Reading
14	Lesson 12 - Reading
15	Lesson 13 – Reading A
16	Lesson 13 – Reading B
17	Lesson 14 - Reading
18	Lesson 15 - Dialogue
19	Lesson 16 - Dialogue
20	Lesson 16 - Reading
21	Lesson 17 - Reading
22	Lesson 18 - Dialogue
23	Lesson 18 - Reading
24	Lesson 19 - Reading
25	Lesson 20 - Dialogue